Thus faith comes from what is heard,
and what is heard comes through the word of Christ.
Romans 10:17

Charley Cook
Corporate Vice President
Kendall Hunt Publishing

Anne P. Battes
Publisher

Mary Sellars Malloy
Project Manager

Mary Wessel
Graphic Designer

GRADE TWO
PARISH EDITION

a Kendall Hunt Company
Cincinnati, Ohio

"The Subcommittee on the Catechism, United States Conference of Catholic Bishops, has found this catechetical series, copyright 2019 to be in conformity with the *Catechism of the Catholic Church.*"

Nihil Obstat Imprimatur

✝ Most Reverend Joseph R. Binzer
Auxiliary Bishop
Vicar General
Archdiocese of Cincinnati
December 7, 2017

The *nihil obstat* and *imprimatur* are official declarations that a book or pamphlet is free of doctrinal and moral error. No implication is contained therein that those who have granted the *nihil obstat* and *imprimatur* agree with the contents, opinions, or statements expressed.

Blest Are We Faith in Action Team

Contributing Writers
Christina De Camp, Kate Sweeney Ristow, Gloria Shahin, Susan Stark
Resources: Marilyn Miller
Revelation: Scripture and Tradition: Rev. Robert J. Hater, PhD
Special Needs: Ann Sherzer
Take Home: Donna N. Glaser
Feasts and Seasons: Ronald C. Lamping, Jo Rotunno

Theological Consultant
Rev. Robert J. Hater, PhD

Editorial Staff
Karen Cain, Project Editor
Elizabeth Shepard, Project Editor
James Spurgin, Editorial Manager
Jo Rotunno, Publisher Emerita

Production Staff
Lori Gray, Graphic Designer
Bob Ishee, Production Manager

Blest Are We Faith & Word Team

Series Authors
Rev. Richard N. Fragomeni, Ph.D.; Maureen Gallagher, Ph.D.; Jeannine Goggin, M.P.S.; Michael P. Horan, Ph.D.

Scripture Co-editor and Consultant
Maria Pascuzzi, S.S.L., S.T.D.

Multicultural Consultant
Angela Erevia, M.C.D.P., M.R.E.

Contributing Writers
Janie Gustafson, Ph.D.
Family Time Scripture: Michael J. Williams, M.S.
Feasts and Seasons: Marianne K. Lenihan
Our Catholic Heritage: Pat Enright

Advisory Board
William C. Allegri, M.A.; Patricia M. Feeley, S.S.J., M.A.; Edmund F. Gordon; Patricia A. Hoffmann; Cris V. Villapando, D.Min.

Consultants
Margaret J. Borders, M.R.S.; Kelly O'Lague Dulka, M.S.W.; Diane Hardick, M.A.; Debra Schurko; Linda S. Tonelli, M.Ed.; Joy Vilotti-Biedrzycki

Music Advisors
GIA Publications: Michael A. Cymbala, Alec Harris, Robert W. Piercy

Acknowledgments
Excerpts from the English translation of the *Roman Missal* © 2010, ICEL. All rights reserved.

Excerpts from *Catholic Household Blessings and Prayers* (revised edition) © 2007, United States Conference of Catholic Bishops, Washington, D.C.

Excerpts from *The New American Bible, Revised Edition* © 2010, 1991, 1986, 1970 Confraternity of Christian Doctrine, Inc., Washington, D.C. Used with permission. All rights reserved. All adaptations of Scripture are based on the *New American Bible, Revised Edition.*

This work is protected by United States copyright laws and is provided *solely for the use of catechists and administrators* in teaching and assessing student learning in their classes. Dissemination or sale of any part of this work (including the World Wide Web) will destroy the integrity of the work and is not permitted.

Music selections copyrighted and/or administered by GIA Publications, Inc., 7404 So. Mason Ave., Chicago, IL 60638.

"Thumb Prayer" adapted from *Catechist* magazine. © Page McKean Zyromski, contributing editor. All content in this publication is protected by copyright. Permission should be obtained from the publisher prior to any prohibited reproduction, storage in a retrieval system, or transmission in any form by any means, electronic, mechanical, photocopying, recording, or otherwise. For information regarding permission(s), write to: Permissions Department, RCL Benziger, 8805 Governor's Hill Drive, Suite 220, Cincinnati, Ohio 45249. Blest Are We® is a trademark of RCL Benziger, a Kendall Hunt Company, or its affiliates.

Copyright © 2019 by RCL Benziger, a Kendall Hunt Company. All Rights Reserved. Printed in the United States of America.

Textbook only:	444443	ISBN: 978-1-5249-4443-8
Textbook with eBook:	444437	ISBN: 978-1-5249-4437-7

1st Printing
December 2017

Contents

Unit 4

Feasts and Seasons

Our Catholic Heritage

Organized according to the four pillars of the Catechism

Let Us Pray

GO TO BlestAreWe.com for Latin texts, Latin pronunciation guides, and Spanish texts for the Sign of the Cross, the Lord's Prayer, the Hail Mary, and the Glory Be.

The Sign of the Cross

In the name of the Father,
and of the Son,
and of the Holy Spirit.
Amen.

The Lord's Prayer

Our Father, who art in heaven,
hallowed be thy name;
thy kingdom come,
thy will be done
on earth as it is in heaven.
Give us this day our daily bread,
and forgive us our trespasses,
as we forgive those who trespass
against us;
and lead us not into temptation,
but deliver us from evil.
Amen.

GO TO BlestAreWe.com for Latin text, Latin pronunciation guides, and Spanish texts for the Sign of the Cross, the Lord's Prayer, the Hail Mary, and the Glory Be.

Pater Noster

Pater noster, qui es in cælis:
sanctificétur nomen tuum;
advéniat regnum tuum;
fiat volúntas tua,
sicut in cælo, et in terra.
Panem nostrum cotidiánum da
nobis hódie;
et dimítte nobis débita nostra,
sicut et nos dimíttimus
debitóribus nostris;
et ne nos indúcas in tentatiónem;
sed líbera nos a malo.
Amen.

Padre Nuestro

Padre nuestro,
que estás en el cielo,
santificado sea tu Nombre;
venga a nosotros tu reino;
hágase tu voluntad
en la tierra
como en el cielo.
Danos hoy nuestro pan de cada día;
perdona nuestras ofensas,
como también nosotros
perdonamos a los que nos
ofenden;
no nos dejes caer en la tentación,
y líbranos del mal.
Amén.

GO TO BlestAreWe.com for Latin text, Latin pronunciation guides, and Spanish texts for the Sign of the Cross, the Lord's Prayer, the Hail Mary, and the Glory Be.

Glory Be

Glory be to the Father
and to the Son
and to the Holy Spirit,
as it was in the beginning
is now, and ever shall be
world without end.
Amen.

The Hail Mary

Hail Mary, full of grace,
the Lord is with thee.
Blessed art thou among women
and blessed is the fruit of thy
womb, Jesus.
Holy Mary, Mother of God,
pray for us sinners,
now and at the hour of our death.
Amen.

Prayer to the Holy Spirit

Come, Holy Spirit, fill the hearts
of your faithful.
And kindle in them the fire of
your love.
Send forth your Spirit and they
shall be created.
And you will renew the face of
the earth.
Amen.

GO TO BlestAreWe.com for Latin text, Latin pronunciation guides, and Spanish texts for the Sign of the Cross, the Lord's Prayer, the Hail Mary, and the Glory Be.

The Nicene Creed

I believe in one God,
the Father almighty,
maker of heaven and earth,
of all things visible and invisible.

I believe in one Lord Jesus Christ,
the Only Begotten Son of God,
born of the Father before all ages.
God from God, Light from Light,
true God from true God,
begotten, not made, consubstantial
with the Father;
through him all things were made.
For us men and for our salvation
he came down from heaven,
and by the Holy Spirit was incarnate
of the Virgin Mary,
and became man.

For our sake he was crucified under
Pontius Pilate,
he suffered death and was buried,
and rose again on the third day
in accordance with the Scriptures.
He ascended into heaven
and is seated at the right hand
of the Father.
He will come again in glory
to judge the living and the dead
and his kingdom will have no end.

I believe in the Holy Spirit, the Lord,
the giver of life,
who proceeds from the Father and
the Son,
who with the Father and the Son is adored
and glorified,
who has spoken through the prophets.

I believe in one, holy, catholic and
apostolic Church.
I confess one Baptism for the forgiveness
of sins
and I look forward to the resurrection of
the dead
and the life of the world to come. Amen.

Roman Missal

Grace Before Meals

Bless us, O Lord, and these thy gifts,
which we are about to receive from
thy bounty,
through Christ our Lord. Amen.

Grace After Meals

We give thee thanks, for all
thy benefits,
almighty God, who lives and
reigns forever. Amen.

Angel of God

Angel of God,
my guardian dear,
to whom God's love commits
me here,
ever this day be at my side,
to light and guard,
to rule and guide.
Amen.

Evening Prayer

Parent: May God bless us and keep us.

Child: **May he guide us in life.**

Parent: May he bless us this evening.

Child: **And keep us in his sight.**

Parent: May God be with you, (name).

Child: **May God be with you, (name).**

Both: In the name of the Father,
and of the Son,
and of the Holy Spirit.
Amen.

Morning Prayer

Loving God, bless the work we do.
Watch over us and guide us
in school and at home.
Help us realize that everything
we do gives praise to you.
We make this prayer in Jesus' name.
Amen.

Act of Contrition

My God,
I am sorry for my sins with
all my heart.
In choosing to do wrong
and failing to do good,
I have sinned against you
whom I should love above all things.
I firmly intend, with your help,
to do penance,
to sin no more,
and to avoid whatever leads me to sin.
Our Savior Jesus Christ
suffered and died for us.
In his name, my God, have mercy.
Amen.

Rite of Penance

My Prayer to Jesus in the Eucharist

The Bible

"My sheep hear my voice;
I know them, and they follow me."

John 10:27

The Bible

God is the author of the Bible. The Bible is God's Word written by human writers. This holy book helps us learn about God's great love for us. Many people wrote the Bible. The Holy Spirit guided all writers of the Bible.

The Bible is also called **Sacred Scripture**. There are readings from Scripture at Mass.

The Old Testament

The Old Testament has stories about people who lived on Earth before Jesus. It tells the story of creation. It tells about Moses and the Ten Commandments.

The New Testament

The New Testament tells about the life and teachings of Jesus. It begins with a **Gospel**. The word *Gospel* means "good news." There are four Gospels. They are named for four followers of Jesus—Matthew, Mark, Luke, and John.

The Bible teaches us how to act as children of God.

ACTIVITY

What is your favorite story from the Bible?
Write or draw a picture about it.

The Life of Jesus

Bethlehem **Wise men** **Nazareth** **Temple** **fishermen** **Cross**

Jesus was born in  .

 went to Bethlehem to see Jesus.

Jesus grew up i  .

At Jerusalem, Jesus taught in the  .

Jesus asked  follow him.

Jesus died on the  near Jerusalem.

Look at the map on the next page. It shows places where Jesus lived and taught.

The Holy Land
in the Time of Jesus
N
W
E
S
Mediterranean Sea
GALILEE
Sea of
Galilee
Nazareth
SAMARIA
River Jordan
Jerusalem
Bethlehem
Dead
Sea
JUDEA

Blest Are We

Words and Music by David Haas
Spanish translation by Ronald F. Krisman

2. For the poor, the meek and the lowly:
We are called, called to serve!
For the weak, the sick and the hungry:
We are called, called to serve!

3. For all those who yearn for freedom:
We are called, called to serve!
For the world, to be God's kingdom:
We are called, called to serve!

2. Por los pobres, los mansos y humildes:
¡Somos llamados para servir!
Por los enfermos, hambrientos, y débiles:
¡Somos llamados para servir!

3. Por los que sufren y quieren ser librados:
¡Somos llamados para servir!
Venga a nosotros el Reino de los Cielos:
¡Somos llamados para servir!

© 2003, GIA Publications, Inc

We Gather as Believers

Unit 1

Our parish community comes together each week. We give praise and thanks to God and we celebrate our faith.

It is good to give thanks to the LORD,
to sing praise to your name, Most High, . . .

Psalm 92:2

King David gave thanks to God through joyful song. We gather in church to sing our praise and thanks to God.

Unit 1

SONG

You Have Put On Christ

Music by Howard Hughes

© 1977, ICEL.

Getting ready for Chapter 1

Take Home

Our Church Welcomes Us

The chapters in Unit 1 focus on membership in the Catholic Church. This first chapter explains being welcomed into the community of believers and being a small part of something larger.

ACTIVITY **Plant a Vine**

With your child, plant a vine such as ivy in a flowerpot, or buy one already planted. Help your child name the parts of the plant (roots, stems, and leaves) and then explain that these small parts make up the whole plant.

THROUGH THE WEEK

A PRAYER FOR THE WEEK O God, we ask that we may be open to others, welcoming them into our Church. Help us to learn from Saint Matthew how to follow you. Amen.

ON SUNDAY
Show hospitality to others. As you go into church, greet the people around you and make them feel welcome.

ON THE WEB
BlestAreWe.com
RCLBLectionary.com
SaintsResource.com

Saint Matthew (first century)

Saint Matthew was an Apostle of Jesus and a Gospel writer. When Jesus asked Matthew, known as Levi, to follow him, Matthew left his job as a tax collector to do so.

Patron Saint of: accountants and bankers

Feast Day: September 21

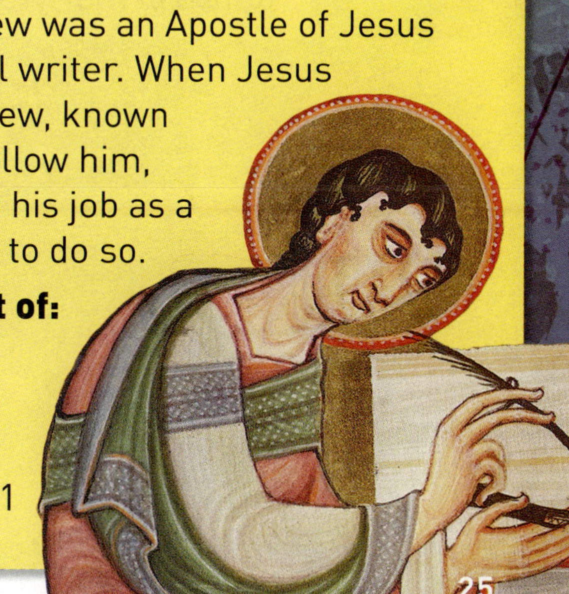

Take Home

Scripture Background
In the Time of Jesus

Homes in the Holy Land Some homes in the Holy Land were quite small, with only a single room. Other larger homes featured one room the width of the house with three long rooms stemming from it. Houses that were two stories high had outside stairs to the second floor. The flat roofs were often made of branches mixed with mud or straw. Wealthy people such as Levi the tax collector, later known as Matthew, may have had larger and possibly more ornate homes.

You can read about a banquet Levi hosted in Luke 5:27–32.

Our Catholic Tradition in Design

Altar Tables In the early Church the Eucharist was celebrated around a table, usually as a shared meal. During the persecutions of early Christians, the Eucharist was often celebrated using the tombs of martyrs as altar tables.

During the Middle Ages, permanent altars became quite ornate and looked more like monuments than tables for a sacred meal.

Twentieth-century reforms inspired by the Second Vatican Council called for the altar to take the form of a table around which the People of God could gather for the Eucharistic feast.

Our Church Welcomes Us

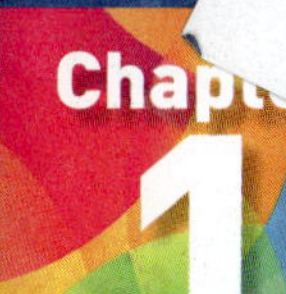

God our Father,
you have brought us here together
so that we can give you thanks and praise . . .

Eucharistic Prayer for Masses with Children I

Share

A community is a place where you feel welcomed.
In a family, people share life and love.
In a neighborhood, people live near each other.
In a classroom, people learn together.

What communities make you feel welcome?

1. I belong to the ______________________ family.
2. I belong to ______________________ Parish.

In what ways is a Catholic parish welcoming?

Hear and Believe Scripture

A Warm Welcome

One day, Jesus met a man who collected taxes. His name was Levi. Jesus asked, "Levi, will you follow me?"

"Yes," Levi answered. He was happy to become a follower of Jesus.

That night, Levi invited his friends and Jesus to a dinner in his home. Jesus was the guest of honor. Levi made all his guests feel welcome.

Based on Luke 5:27–29

Scripture Verse
. . . "Follow me."
Luke 5:27

God's People

Today we welcome others like Levi did. As baptized followers of Jesus we are open to everyone. We are the **People of God**, the Church. We celebrate a holy meal together at **Mass**. This holy meal makes present again Jesus' sacrifice on the Cross.

Our Church Teaches

There is one way all the People of God are alike. We are followers of Jesus Christ. We welcome all who believe in Jesus. Our parish is a community that worships, works, and prays together. We welcome all people.

We Believe

We are the People of God, the Church. We celebrate all who believe in Jesus.

Faith Words

People of God
The People of God are followers of Jesus Christ.

Mass
The Mass is a holy meal Jesus shares with us. At Mass, we offer praise and sacrifice to God and can receive the Body and Blood of Jesus.

In what ways do Church members show they are People of God?

Respond Welcome, Neighbors!

Tommy and his family came to the United States to escape a war in their country. Soldiers had put them out of their home.

Father Louis and the people of St. John's Parish want to help. The family will live in a house that belongs to the church. A teacher is helping Tommy's family learn English. Some parish families are bringing them food and clothes. Others will bring books and toys. Father Louis is helping Tommy's parents find jobs.

How are the people of St. John's Parish showing that they are the People of God?

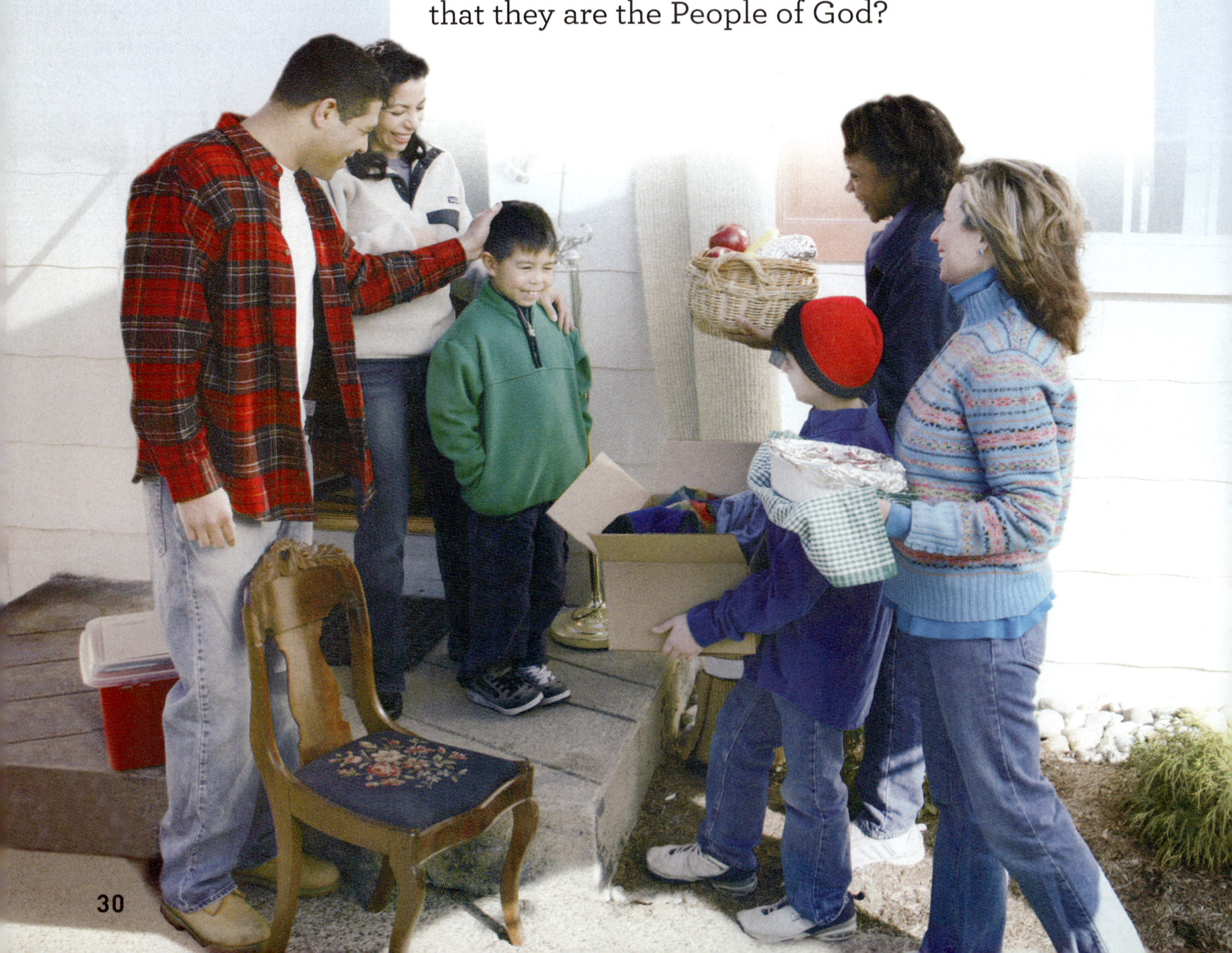

ACTIVITIES

1. In the box, draw a picture of someone who is caring for others.

2. Talk about ways to make other people feel welcome.

When do we celebrate being the People of God?

A Prayer of Thanksgiving

We celebrate the People of God when we pray together.

Leader: Sing with joy to God! Be glad to serve the Lord.

All: **We are the People of God.**

Leader: God made us. God calls us together as one Church.

All: **We are the People of God.**

Leader: Give thanks to God, who is always good. Be joyful, for God's kindness lasts forever.

All: **We are the People of God. Amen.**

Based on Psalm 100

Scripture Verse
Give thanks to him,
bless his name; . . .
Psalm 100:4

Chapter Review 1

A **Circle** the correct answer.

1. We _____ together as the People of God.

   pray   run   travel

2. Our Church _____ all people.

   forgets   knows   welcomes

3. The Mass celebrates God's _____ for us.

   love   need   worry

4. As Catholics, we are all followers of _____.

   Jean   Jesus   John

B **Write** what we are called to do as the People of God.

As the People of God, we are called to

____

____

Faith in Action

Sharing Hospitality Some families belong to a parish welcoming committee. They greet people as they come to Mass. They help new families learn about parish activities. They even help visitors to feel welcome.

In Everyday Life

ACTIVITY Think about ways that you can make someone feel welcome. In the space below, draw a picture of one way you would do this at home, at school, or in your neighborhood.

In Your Parish

ACTIVITY Make a welcome badge like the one pictured to wear as a parish greeter.

Getting ready for Chapter 2

Take Home

Baptism

This chapter describes the journey your child has begun in the faith. Baptism uses common elements, such as water, light, and oil as signs of our membership in the Catholic Church.

ACTIVITY **Signs of Baptism**

Show pictures of Baptisms of family members. Discuss the signs of white garment, holy water, Sacred Chrism, and the baptismal candle. Share stories about the experience.

THROUGH THE WEEK

A PRAYER FOR THE WEEK Jesus, we are grateful to be your followers. We know that belonging to your Church will bring us happiness and blessings. Amen.

ON SUNDAY

Upon entering church, dip your fingers in the holy water font and make the Sign of the Cross. Remember you are a follower of Jesus.

ON THE WEB

BlestAreWe.com

RCLBLectionary.com

SaintsResource.com

Saint Josephine Bakhita (1868–1947)

Not everyone is baptized as an infant. As a child living in Sudan, Josephine Bakhita was sold into slavery. She was later sent to Italy, where she worked for a Catholic family. After learning about Jesus she was baptized, and in 1896 she became a religious sister.

Patron Saint of: Sudan

Feast Day: February 8

Take Home

Scripture Background
Before the Time of Jesus

Baptism In the Old Testament, *baptism* was a term signifying Jewish ritual cleansing or purification. John the Baptist preached a baptism of repentance for the forgiveness of sins. With Jesus' Death and Resurrection, baptism took on a different meaning. Through the Sacrament of Baptism, Christians are born again through water and the Holy Spirit. They enter into the Death and Resurrection of Jesus and rise to new life in him, thereby becoming adoptive sons of the Father. Christian Baptism fills us with sanctifying grace, the free gift of God's life in us. Baptism cleanses us from the effects of Original Sin and all personal sin committed before Baptism.

You can read about John the Baptist's baptism of repentance in Mark 1:1–11.

Our Catholic Tradition in Art

The Baptism of Christ *The Baptism of Christ* by Piero della Francesca now hangs in the National Gallery in London, but it was originally an altarpiece in the chapel of Saint John the Baptist in Piero's native town, Sansepolcro, in central Italy.

The painting illustrates the artist's concept of Christ's Baptism, with John the Baptist pouring water over Christ as the Holy Spirit descends from Heaven.

Baptism

Chapter 2

We are children of the light.
We are children of the day.

Based on 1 Thessalonians 5:5

Share

People have many ways to show they belong to a group.

Look at these pictures. Match each sign of belonging with its group. Then tell about a sign of belonging that you have.

Sign

What signs of belonging do Church members have?

Hear and Believe **Worship**

The Sacrament of Baptism

The **Sacraments** are special signs that help us celebrate our life in the Catholic Church. They bring us God's gift of grace. **Grace** is the gift of God's life within us that fills us with his love.

The first Sacrament we receive is **Baptism**. Baptism puts a permanent character, or mark, on our souls. We can only receive it one time.

The very first people God created disobeyed him. Their names are Adam and Eve. Their sin is called **Original Sin**. Baptism takes away Original Sin and all sin. In Baptism we are united with Jesus Christ, who came to forgive sins.

1 Two things must happen in the celebration of Baptism. The priest or deacon must pour blessed water three times over the person's head while saying, "I baptize you in the name of the Father, and of the Son, and of the Holy Spirit."

The symbolic actions that follow in the celebration of Baptism include the following.

2 The priest or deacon makes the Sign of the Cross on the baby's forehead with Sacred Chrism. Sacred Chrism is one of the three holy oils used by the Church.

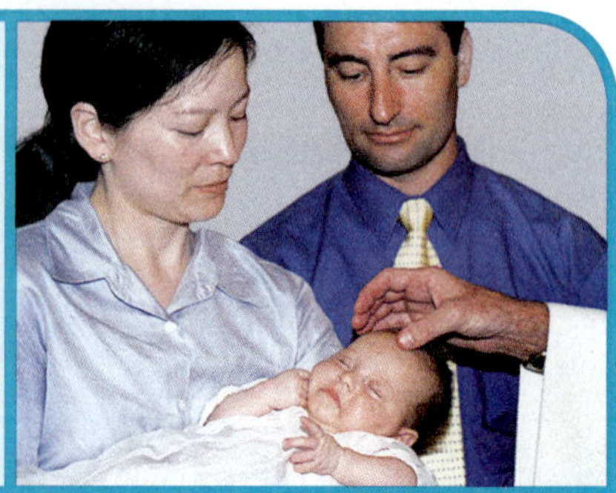

3 The person receives a white garment. The priest or deacon says, "You have become a new creation, and have clothed yourself in Christ."

4 The godparents or parents receive a lighted candle. The priest or deacon says, "Receive the light of Christ."

Based on the *Rite of Baptism for Children*

Signs of New Life

We are welcomed as members of the Church at Baptism. The special signs of Baptism remind us that we share in the life of Christ.

Our Church Teaches

A bishop, priest, or deacon is the usual minister of Baptism. If needed, anyone can baptize with the triple pouring of water and the words of the Sacrament. The person must also want to do what the Church does in Baptism. Through Baptism, we become the children of God. We receive the Holy Spirit.

We Believe

In Baptism we begin our new lives as members of the Catholic Church.

Faith Words

Sacraments
Sacraments are special signs of God's love and presence that bring us his grace.

grace
Grace is the gift of God's life within us that fills us with his love.

Baptism
The Sacrament of Baptism washes away sin and welcomes new members to the Church.

Original Sin
Original Sin is the sin of the first man and woman, Adam and Eve.

In what ways do we show we belong to the Catholic Church?

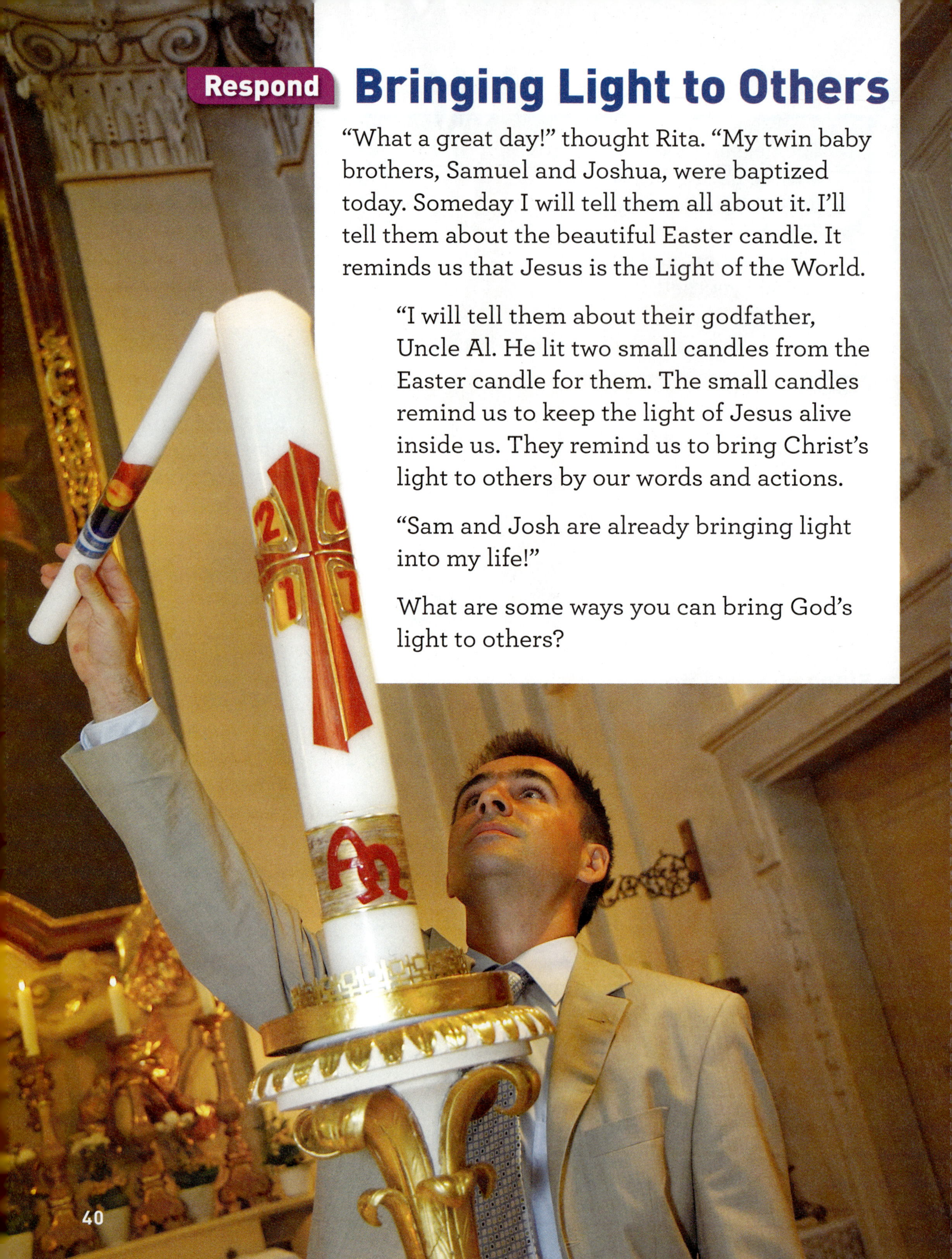

Respond

Bringing Light to Others

"What a great day!" thought Rita. "My twin baby brothers, Samuel and Joshua, were baptized today. Someday I will tell them all about it. I'll tell them about the beautiful Easter candle. It reminds us that Jesus is the Light of the World.

"I will tell them about their godfather, Uncle Al. He lit two small candles from the Easter candle for them. The small candles remind us to keep the light of Jesus alive inside us. They remind us to bring Christ's light to others by our words and actions.

"Sam and Josh are already bringing light into my life!"

What are some ways you can bring God's light to others?

ACTIVITY

Use these words to complete the puzzle.

belonging	Light	Sacrament
children	Water	Sin

Down

1. Baptism takes away Original ________ and all sin.
2. Baptism is a sign of ________ to the Church.
4. ________ is used in Baptism.

Across

3. We are ________ of God.
5. A ________ is a sign of God's love.
6. Jesus is the ________ of the World.

In what ways can we celebrate that we are God's children?

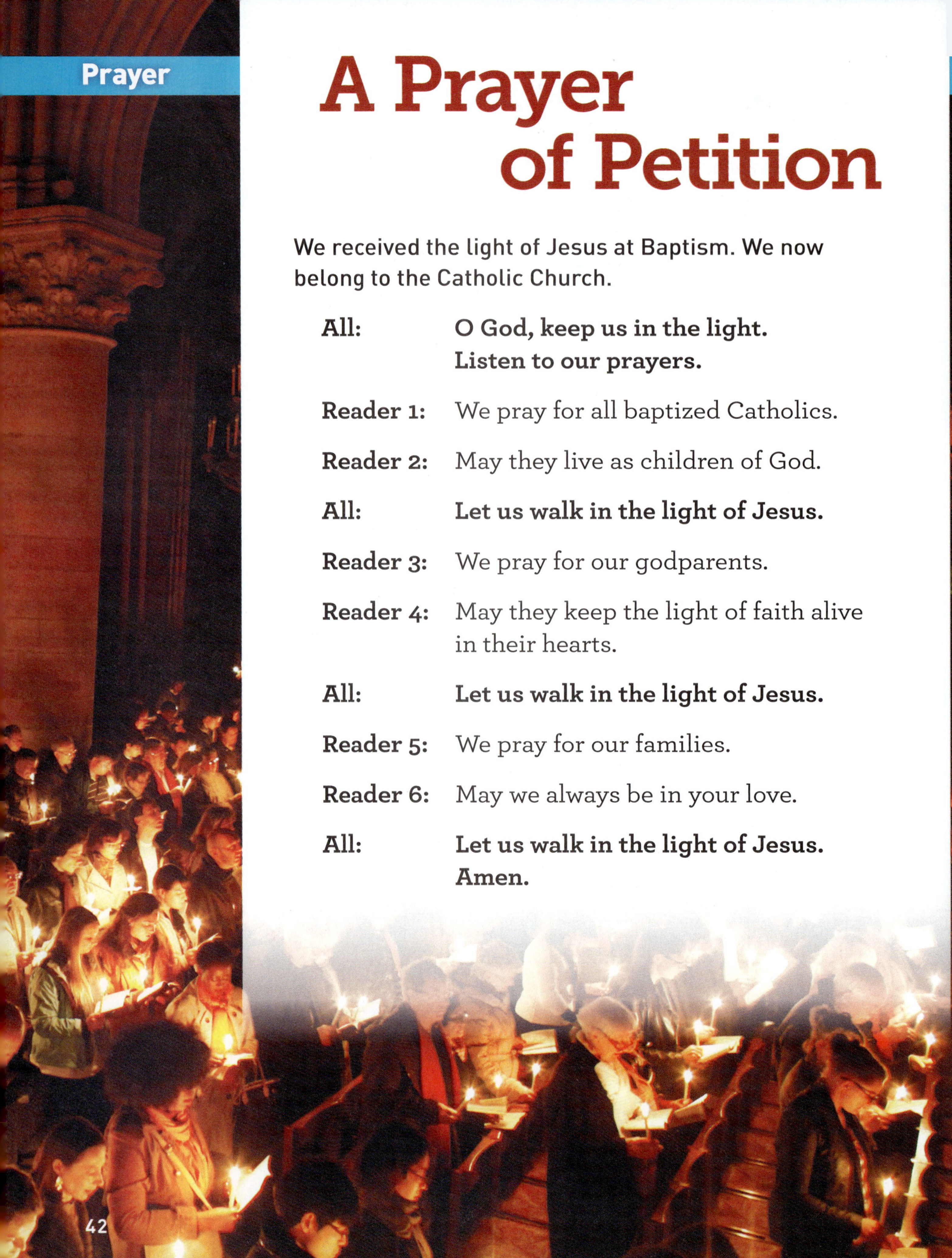

A Prayer of Petition

We received the light of Jesus at Baptism. We now belong to the Catholic Church.

All: **O God, keep us in the light. Listen to our prayers.**

Reader 1: We pray for all baptized Catholics.

Reader 2: May they live as children of God.

All: **Let us walk in the light of Jesus.**

Reader 3: We pray for our godparents.

Reader 4: May they keep the light of faith alive in their hearts.

All: **Let us walk in the light of Jesus.**

Reader 5: We pray for our families.

Reader 6: May we always be in your love.

All: **Let us walk in the light of Jesus. Amen.**

Chapter Review 2

A **Draw** the one thing that must be used in the Sacrament of Baptism. Then draw one of the three other things that are used in the celebration of Baptism.

B **Draw a line** to match the descriptions with the correct words.

1. A celebration of God's love and presence •	• Holy Spirit
2. The sin of Adam and Eve •	• children of God
3. Who we receive at Baptism •	• Sacrament
4. What we become at Baptism •	• Original Sin

Faith in Action

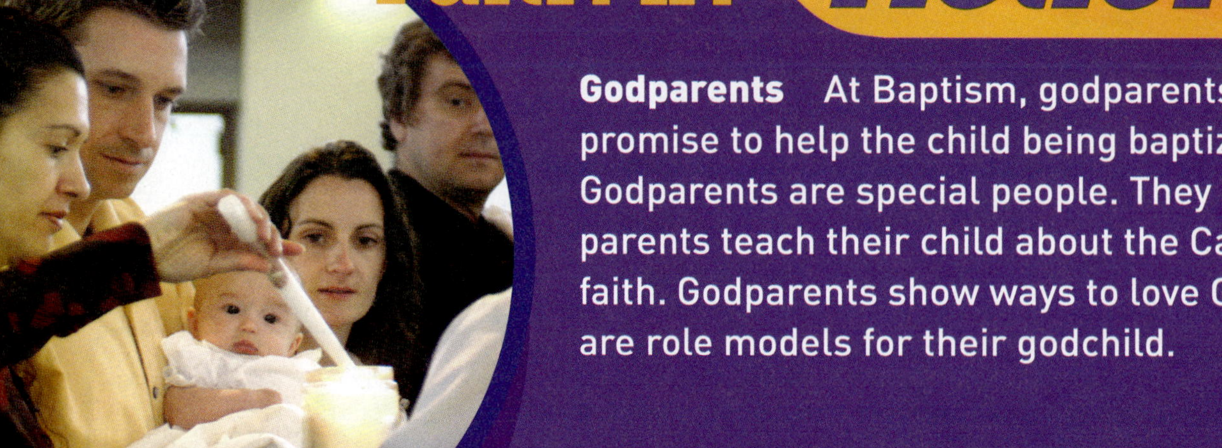

Godparents At Baptism, godparents promise to help the child being baptized. Godparents are special people. They help parents teach their child about the Catholic faith. Godparents show ways to love God. They are role models for their godchild.

In Everyday Life

ACTIVITY

Write a thank-you note to your godparents.

In Your Parish

ACTIVITY

Have you attended a Baptism in your parish? If so, who was there? What do you remember most about the celebration?

Take Home

Our Church Shows Us How to Live

Jesus shows us how to live in a way that pleases God. The saints have also shown us different ways to live a life that is holy. They lived very different lives, but had three things in common. They tried to live by the Commandments, they loved God, and they loved their neighbors.

ACTIVITY **Family Saints**

Together, pick out an admirable quality or virtue possessed by each family member. Make a badge for each family "saint" with the person's name and virtue. Then wear your badges this week during family meals.

THROUGH THE WEEK

A PRAYER FOR THE WEEK We thank you, God, for giving us Saint Peter Claver, who showed us how to live a life of Christian charity. Give us the strength and courage to follow his example. Amen.

ON SUNDAY
Are there statues of saints in your church? Name at least two saints whose images you see in church.

ON THE WEB
BlestAreWe.com
RCLBLectionary.com
SaintsResource.com

Saint Peter Claver (1581–1654)

Peter Claver was a Spanish Jesuit missionary. He devoted his life and ministry to serving African slaves transported to South America. He often lived in the same crowded and unhealthy conditions as the people in his care.

Patron Saint of: interracial justice

Feast Day: September 9

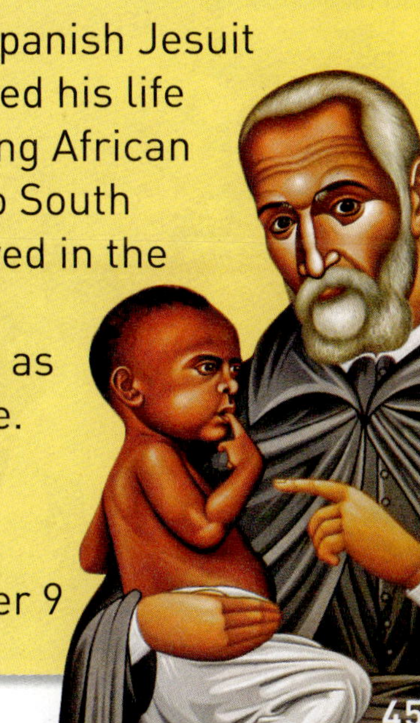

Take Home

Scripture Background
In the Time of Jesus

Samaritans Samaritans lived in Israel around Mount Gerizin. Jews disliked Samaritans. Although sharing a common heritage with Jews, Samaritans had different religious customs. Jesus taught a parable involving a Samaritan who stopped to help a wounded Jew when other fellow Jews did not. He also spoke of a Samaritan leper as the only grateful one of ten lepers cured. Jesus' message is that the Kingdom of God is for all people.

You can read about Samaritans in Luke 17:11–19 and about the Good Samaritan in Luke 10:29–35.

Our Catholic Tradition in Law

Good Samaritan Law The story of the Good Samaritan is famous. Many people know about the kind man who stopped to help the hurt stranger. The story is so famous that a Good Samaritan law has been enacted. This law requires people who have medical training to stop and help when they see an accident.

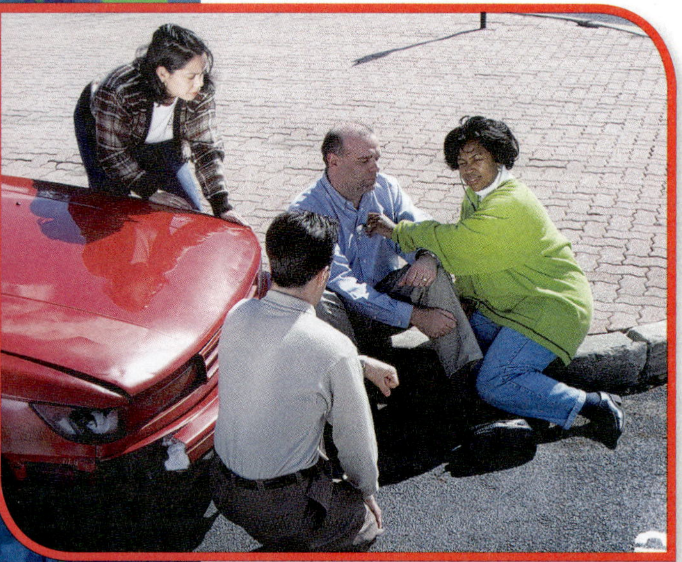

There was a time when those who had medical training wouldn't stop because they were afraid of being sued. This law protects the Good Samaritans from being sued, while requiring them to use their training to help the injured.

Our Church Shows Us How to Live

Chapter 3

Love one another. Then everyone will know that you are my followers. *Based on* John 13:35

Share

Some people are heroes. They help others. They show us how to live.

ACTIVITY

Find the heroes in these pictures. Draw circles around them.

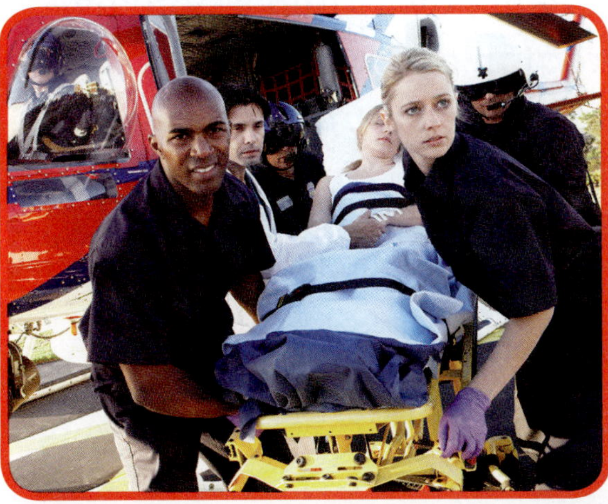

Who is your favorite real-life hero? Why?

Who are the Church's heroes?

Hear and Believe **Scripture**

The Real Hero

One day, Jesus told a story about a hero.

A man was traveling by himself. Robbers attacked him. They beat him and took his money. He was left lying in the road, badly hurt.

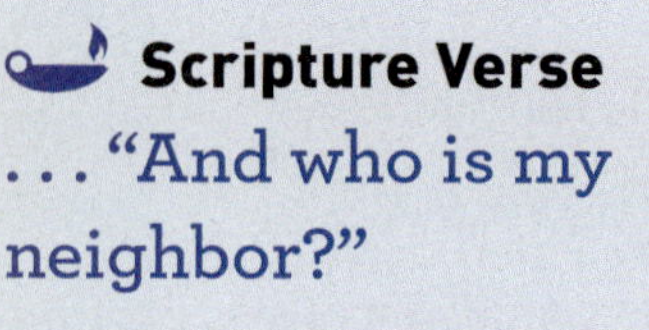

Scripture Verse

. . . "And who is my neighbor?"

Luke 10:29

Soon a religious leader came by. He saw the man, but he just kept going.

Next, a man who worked in the Temple came along. He also passed by without helping.

Then, a third man came by, riding a donkey. He was from the region of Samaria. He saw the hurt man on the road. He stopped at once. He washed the man's wounds. He put bandages on them. Then the man from Samaria put the hurt man on the donkey. He took him to an inn. There he paid the innkeeper to care for the man.

Based on Luke 10:29–35

Heroes of Our Church

The Church has many heroes. Some are like the good man from Samaria. The Church also has **saints** like Mary, the Mother of Jesus. Saints showed great love for God and others and died filled with God's grace. They live with him now in Heaven. These Church heroes teach us how to act like Jesus.

Our Church Teaches

All people are made to be **holy**. To be holy is to be like God. Through Baptism we are called to live good and holy lives.

We Believe

God calls us to be holy. We grow in holiness by loving God and by loving other people.

Faith Words

saints
Saints are people who show great love for other people and for God.

holy
To be holy means to be like God.

In what ways can we imitate Mary and all the saints?

Respond Mary and Other Saints

Mary and other saints teach us how to live as Christians.

Mary is the greatest saint of all. She was a good mother to Jesus. She teaches us to trust God and to care for others.

Saint Peter Claver cared for people no one else cared about. He teaches us to reach out in love to everyone in need.

Saint Brigid sold what she had. She gave the money to people who were poor. She teaches us to share our blessings with others.

Saint Jerome loved to teach people how to read and understand the Bible. He teaches us to share the Word of God with others.

The Church has many heroes like these. They all teach us how to love God and follow Jesus.

Which saint is your favorite? How can you follow this saint's example?

ACTIVITY

Draw a picture of someone you know who is a hero.
Or, draw a picture of yourself acting in a good and holy way.

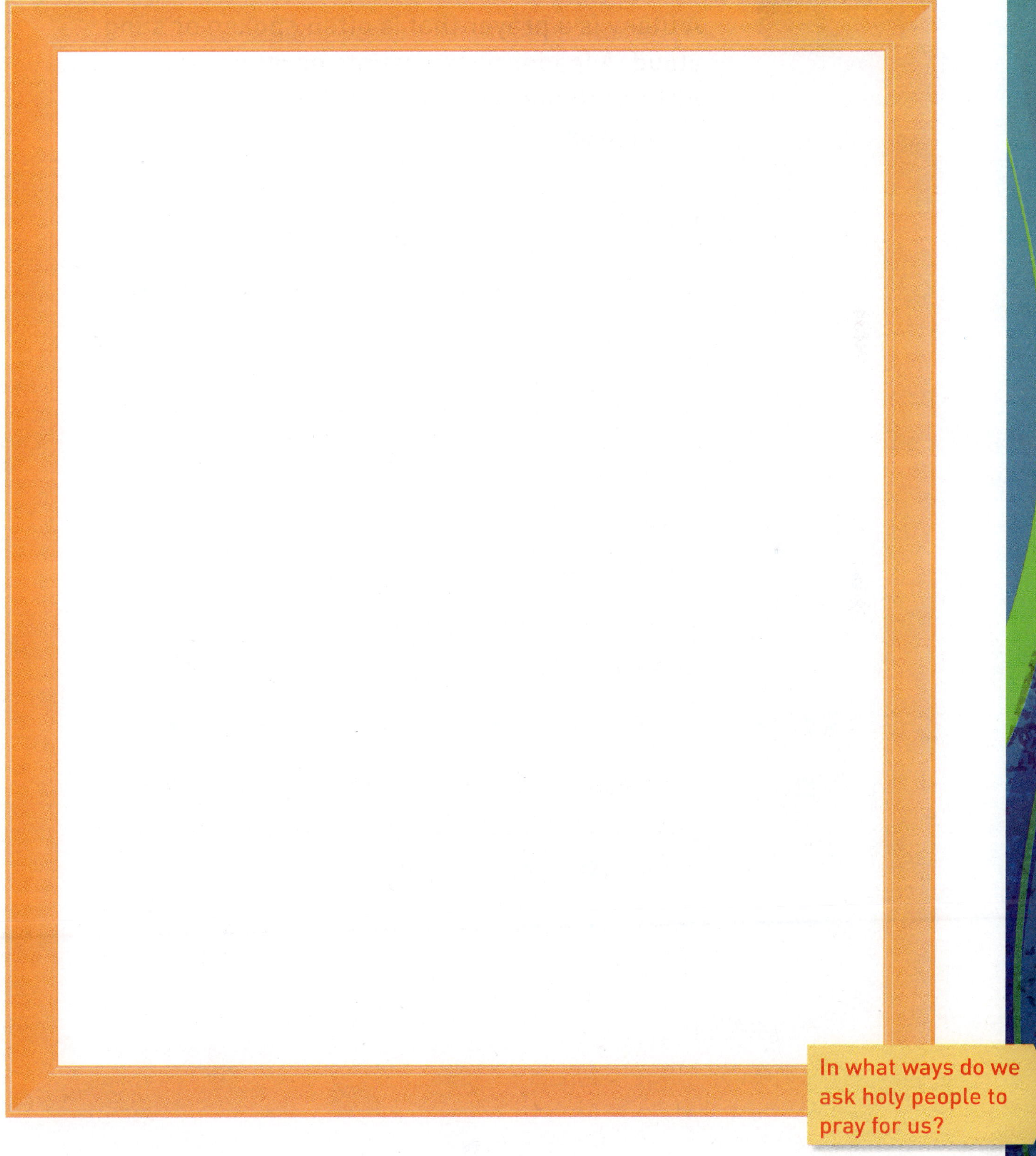

In what ways do we ask holy people to pray for us?

Praying a Litany

A litany is a prayer that is often spoken or sung aloud. A leader names saints or other holy people. After each one, we ask the saint or holy person to pray for us.

Leader:	**All:**
Holy Mary, Mother of God,	**pray for us.**
Saint Peter Claver,	**pray for us.**
Saint Brigid,	**pray for us.**
Saint Jerome,	**pray for us.**
All who helped the poor and the hungry,	**pray for us.**
All who cared for the weak and the sick,	**pray for us.**
All holy men and women,	**pray for us.**

All: Holy God, may we follow the example of your saints and other holy people. May we always try to help people in need. Amen.

Chapter Review 3

A **Circle** the words to complete the sentences.

1. People who show great love for others and for God are ______.

   old　　saints　　selfish

2. To be like God is to be ______.

   holy　　pretty　　rich

3. We become holy by loving ______ and other people.

   God　　stories　　things

4. In Jesus' story, the hero who helped a hurt man was a ______.

   priest　　tax collector　　man from Samaria

B **Draw or write about** a good and holy action that you will do to follow Jesus.

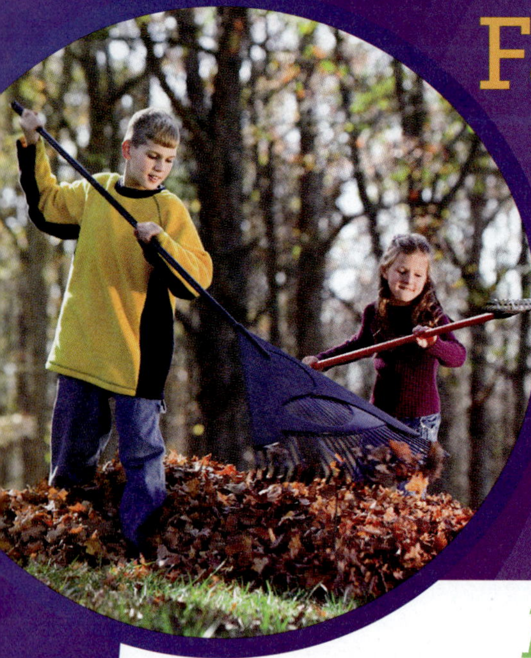

Faith in Action

Helping Hands Ministry People in this ministry serve people who need help with tasks. Someone may need help to replace a ceiling light bulb or to recycle newspapers. Members may read letters to neighbors with poor vision. They reach out to anyone who needs a helping hand.

In Everyday Life

ACTIVITY What should you do? Place the number of the problem in front of the best answer.

1. A group makes fun of a teacher.
2. You see an older boy grab the lunch of a younger boy.
3. You have a friend who is a bully.

_____ Ask yourself if you want that kind of friend.

_____ Report what you see to an adult.

_____ Do not laugh with them.

In Your Parish

ACTIVITY Name two ways that people in your parish treat others with kindness.

____

____

Getting ready for Chapter 4

Take Home

We Praise and Thank God

Saint Augustine said those who sing pray twice. He was telling us that raising our voices in song pleases God. This chapter presents the value of song as a form of prayer and the value of prayers of thanks and praise.

ACTIVITY **Name That Hymn**

Play "Name That Hymn!" with your family. You can hum, play a musical instrument, or sing "la-la-la" to the tune of a favorite hymn. Let the others guess the title. Then invite them to sing along, if they know the words.

THROUGH THE WEEK

A PRAYER FOR THE WEEK Thank you, Lord, for giving us life. May we use our voices to sing thanks and praise to you. Amen.

ON SUNDAY

Singing is a key way we participate in the Mass. Be a family who sings! As Saint Augustine said, when we sing we pray twice.

ON THE WEB

BlestAreWe.com
RCLBLectionary.com
SaintsResource.com

Pope Saint Gregory the Great (c. 540–604)

As pope, Gregory the Great reformed the Church and gave generously to the poor. Pope Gregory I helped bring Christianity to England. He is credited with initiating a solemn form of singing called Gregorian chant.

Patron Saint of: singers and musicians

Feast Day: September 3

Take Home

Scripture Background
Before the Time of Jesus

Psalms The Book of Psalms is an Old Testament collection of 150 songs, laments, and other types of prayers. Psalms have varied intentions: some glorify God, some offer praise and thanksgiving, some are wisdom psalms, others are petitions or laments, and still others are historical. David is considered to be the author of many of the psalms. Because some of the psalms were also written after David's death, they can be considered a record of the Israelites' existence over time.

You can read Psalms 92 and 149 as examples of psalms of thanksgiving and praise.

Our Catholic Tradition in Music

Gregorian Chant Since the sixth century the Church has been expressing its praise of God musically through Gregorian chant. Named after Pope Gregory I, chant is a solemn form of singing that creates a harmony between words and melody. Because in some pagan religions music was used to stir up people, Christians were encouraged to have a kind of music that was prayerful. Gregorian chant met that standard. There were other kinds of chants before Gregorian chant, but it was more beautiful and developed than some of the others.

Contemporary recordings of Gregorian chant have brought an appreciation of this prayer form to a wider audience.

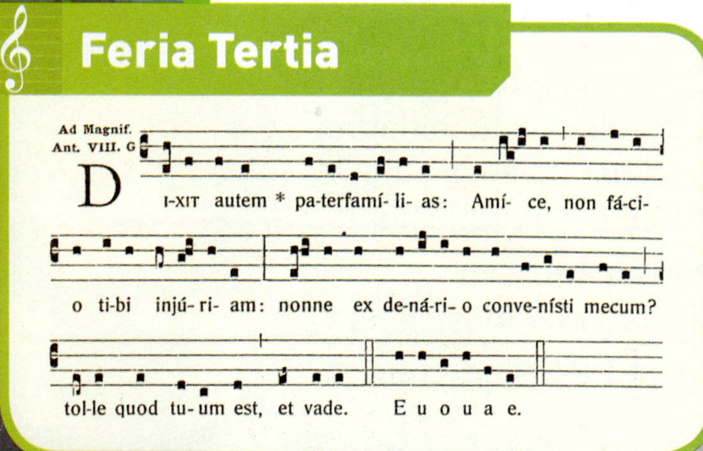

We Praise and Thank God

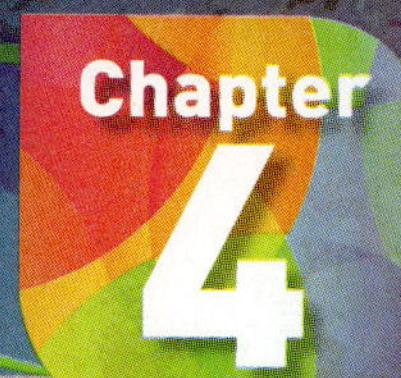

Sing to the LORD a new song, . . . Psalm 149:1

Share

Celebrations are important times. People come together to give thanks. They say thank you for special people or gifts.

On the Fourth of July we give thanks for freedom.

On birthdays we give thanks for life.

On Thanksgiving we give thanks for all our blessings.

On Christmas we give thanks for the birth of Jesus.

1. Write the name of a celebration you enjoyed.

____

2. Write why you gave thanks.

____

____

Why do God's people give thanks?

Hear and Believe Scripture

King David Gives Thanks

King David loved God. He liked to lead the Jewish people in prayer. David liked to play the harp, dance, and sing. He sang about God's goodness. He thanked God for giving the people many gifts.

One day Jewish leaders brought the Ark that held God's laws into David's city. David ordered musicians to play on their harps, lyres, and cymbals. Then David sang out,

"How good it is to give God thanks and glory!
I sing praise to your name, O God.
Every morning you are kind to me.
You are with me all day and all night.
Your goodness fills me with gladness.
I am happy because of the gifts you give
to me."

Based on 1 Chronicles 15 and Psalm 92:1–5

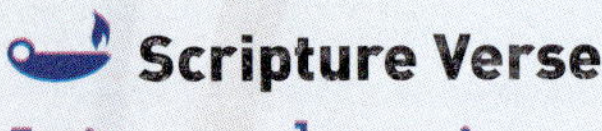

Scripture Verse

It is good to give thanks to the LORD, . . .

Psalm 92:2

We Give Praise and Thanks

King David wrote many song-prayers called **psalms**. Our parish community sings special songs at Mass. We give **praise** and thanks to God with holy music.

Our Church Teaches

Prayer is talking to and listening to God. There are many kinds of prayer. Some prayers give thanks to God. Some prayers give praise for God's goodness. We can pray alone. We can pray with others. We can sing or play music as we pray.

We Believe

We can pray through songs or dancing, or by listening to holy music. Holy music helps us give praise and thanks to God.

Faith Words

psalms
Psalms are prayers from the Bible that are often sung.

praise
Praise is a joyful type of prayer. It celebrates God's goodness.

prayer
Prayer is talking to and listening to God.

What are some ways we praise and thank God?

Respond Glory to God

In the first part of the Mass we usually sing "Glory to God." This special song is called the Gloria. It is a prayer of praise and thanks. This is how it begins.

Glory to God in the highest,
and on earth peace to people of good will.

We praise you,
we bless you,
we adore you,
we glorify you,
we give you thanks for your great glory,
Lord God, heavenly King,
O God, almighty Father.

Roman Missal

What songs do you sing at Mass?

ACTIVITY

1. Write your own prayer of praise.

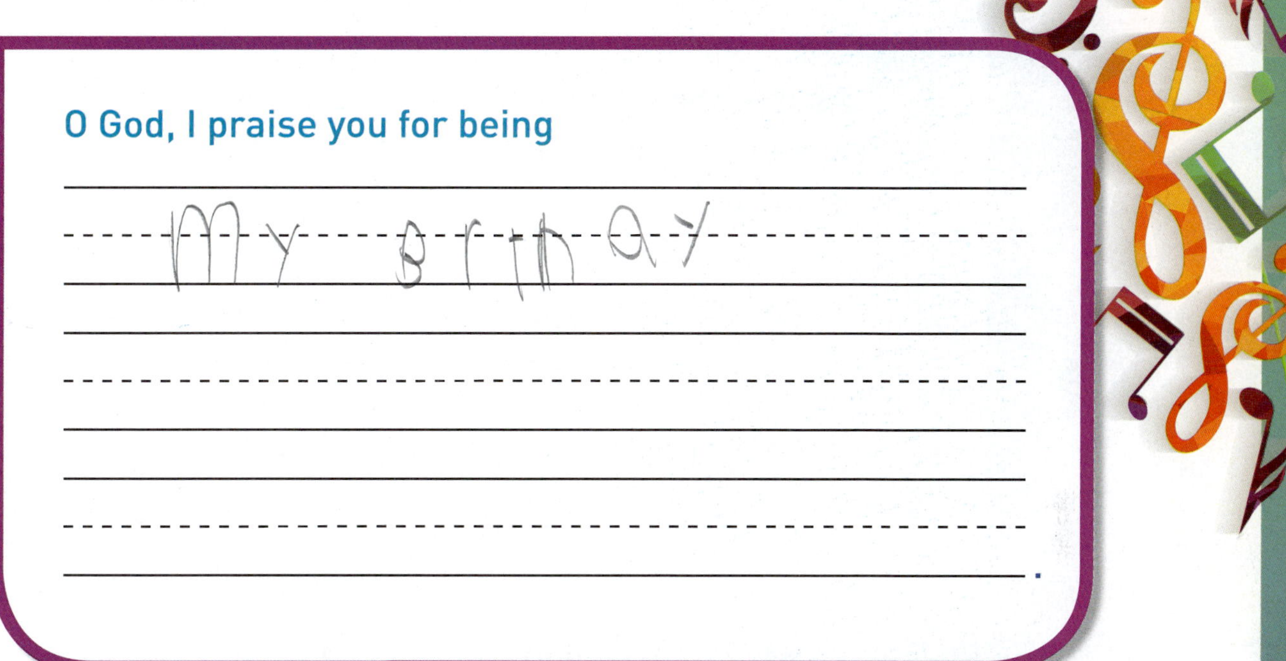

2. Write your own prayer of thanks.

O God, I thank you for

You will use these prayers in the prayer celebration.

In what way can I praise and thank God with song?

A Prayer of Praise and Thanks

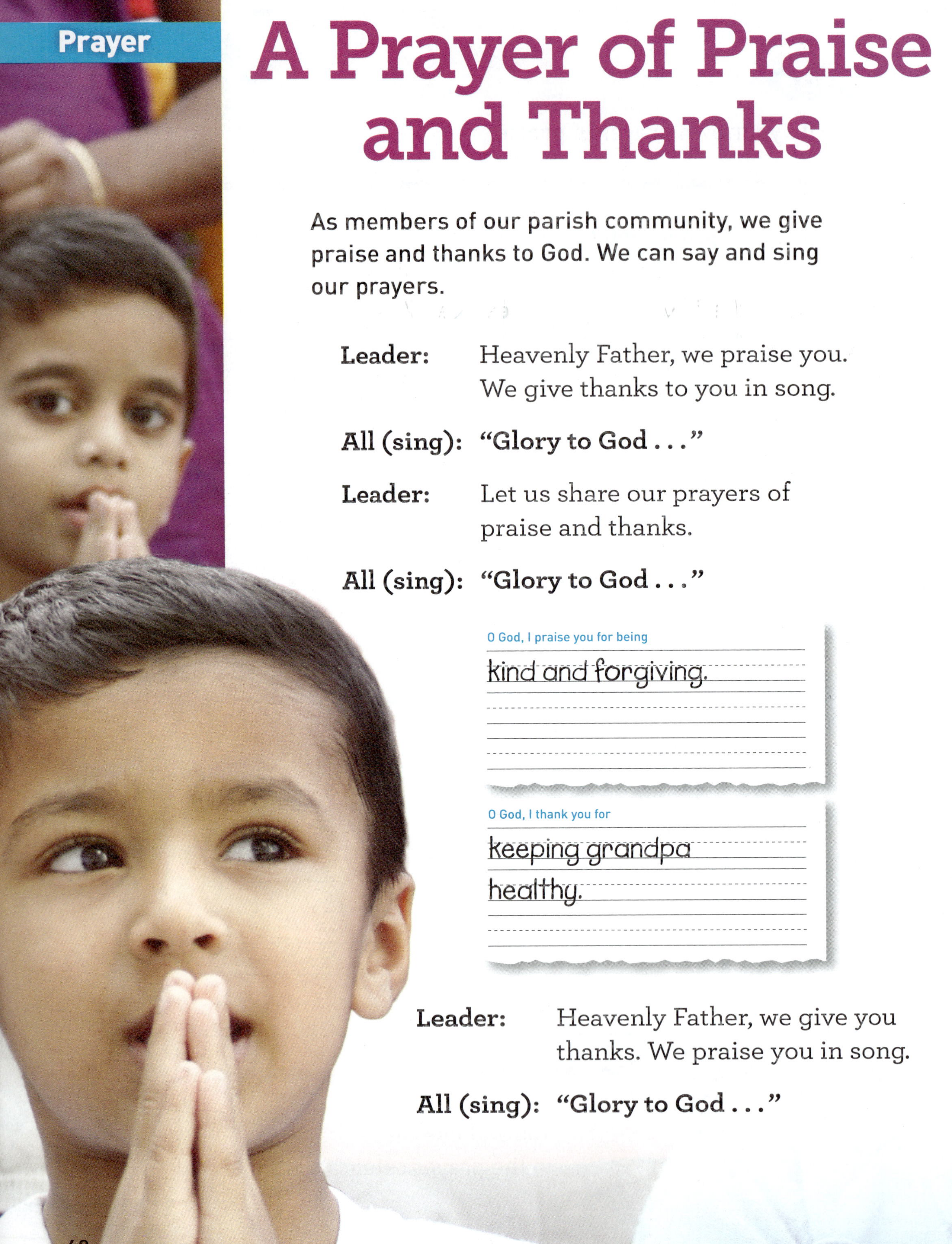

As members of our parish community, we give praise and thanks to God. We can say and sing our prayers.

Leader: Heavenly Father, we praise you. We give thanks to you in song.

All (sing): "Glory to God . . ."

Leader: Let us share our prayers of praise and thanks.

All (sing): "Glory to God . . ."

O God, I praise you for being

kind and forgiving.

O God, I thank you for

keeping grandpa healthy.

Leader: Heavenly Father, we give you thanks. We praise you in song.

All (sing): "Glory to God . . ."

Chapter Review

A Think about the story King David Gives Thanks. **Draw a line** under the words that name the things King David liked to do.

mop the floor	lead people in prayer
sing and dance	run in races
play the harp	give thanks to God

B **Circle** the best answer.

1. What do we call an important time when people come together to give thanks?

   psalm   celebration   ark

2. What is a joyful type of prayer that celebrates God's goodness?

   praise   thanksgiving   sorrow

3. What is the song that we usually sing in the first part of the Mass?

   Amen   Holy, Holy, Holy   Gloria

4. What do we call the prayers that King David wrote?

   psalms   impressions   creeds

Faith in Action

Cantor We can praise God in song. When we sing in church, we often have a music leader called a cantor. A cantor loves to sing praises to God. The cantor leads us in singing holy songs.

In Everyday Life

ACTIVITY Think about holy songs you like to sing. Which song is your favorite? Write down the words you remember.

In Your Parish

ACTIVITY Circle the musical instruments used in your parish.

Unit 2

We Ask God's Forgiveness

God is always ready to forgive us when we sin.
God calls us to be sorry for the wrongs we have done.
He wants us to forgive others who have wronged us.

"... Rejoice with me because I have found my lost sheep."
Luke 15:6

God is like a shepherd who is happy to find his lost sheep. God rejoices when we are sorry for our sins.

Psalm 51: Be Merciful, O Lord

Psalm 51

Music by Marty Haugen

REFRAIN

VERSES

1. Have mercy on me, God, in your kindness,
   in your compassion, blot out my offense.
   O wash me more and more from my guilt and my sorrow,
   and cleanse me from all of my sin.
   Refrain

2. My offenses, truly I know them,
   and my sins are always before me;
   against you alone have I sinned, O Lord,
   what is evil in your sight I have done.
   Refrain

3. Create in me a clean heart, O God,
   put your steadfast spirit in my soul.
   Cast me not away from your presence, O Lord,
   and take not your spirit from me.
   Refrain

4. Give back to me the joy of your salvation,
   let your willing spirit bear me up
   and I shall teach your way to the ones who have wandered,
   and bring them all home to your side.
   Refrain

© 1983, GIA Publications, Inc.; refrain translation © 1969, ICEL.

Getting ready for Chapter 5

Take Home

Choosing Good

How do we figure out what is good and proper? We work to form a correct conscience to help us identify a right understanding of the good and make the proper choice in the first place. The teaching of the Church, reception of the Sacraments, the guidance of trusted friends, mentors, and spiritual advisors, reading, and prayer can assist us in forming a correct conscience. Your child will learn that conscience is our ability to know right from wrong.

ACTIVITY **Pick-Up Sticks**

Play pick-up sticks with your child. Discuss how the game is like making moral choices, because you need to choose carefully in order to succeed.

THROUGH THE WEEK

A PRAYER FOR THE WEEK Lord, thank you for giving us the freedom to choose. Help us to use this gift to make right choices. Help us to be caring like Saint Peter of Saint Joseph Betancur. Amen.

ON SUNDAY
During the Penitential Act of the Mass, reflect on the choices you made during the week. Thank God for his guidance.

ON THE WEB
BlestAreWe.com
RCLBLectionary.com
SaintsResource.com

Saint Peter of Saint Joseph Betancur (1619–1667)

Peter lived as a shepherd in the Canary Islands. At age 31 he went to the New World to serve the people of Guatemala. He took vows as a Third Order Franciscan and opened hospitals, schools, and chapels in Guatemala City.

Patron Saint of: Guatemala

Feast Day: April 18

Take Home

Scripture Background

In the Time of Jesus

Inheritance Israelite tradition held that the eldest son would inherit the property and holdings of the father. The primary aim was to preserve the territory within each clan. Further legislation also established the right of the firstborn to inherit twice as much as his brothers. In the parable of the Forgiving Father, the younger son has already taken his share. So when the elder son is told that all that the father has is his, it literally means everything.

You can read this parable in Luke 15:11–32.

Our Catholic Tradition in Art

Return of the Prodigal Son

The Rembrandt painting *Return of the Prodigal Son* depicts the story Jesus told of the young man who left his family and squandered his fortune. Poor, hungry, and alone, he returned home. As this painting shows, his father welcomed him back as a son, not as a servant.

Henri Nouwen based his book, *The Return of the Prodigal Son*, on Rembrandt's painting.

Choosing Good

Chapter 5

Love the Lord, your God, and obey his word.

Based on Deuteronomy 30:20

Share

We make many choices every day. Some choices are easy, but some are hard. Some are right, but others are wrong.

ACTIVITY

Draw a happy face for each good choice below. Draw a sad face for each poor choice.

1. Tom does not share with his friends.

2. Juanita tells her dad the truth.

3. Wes obeys his mom and turns off the TV.

4. Mary takes a dollar that is not hers.

What helps us to know what is right and wrong?

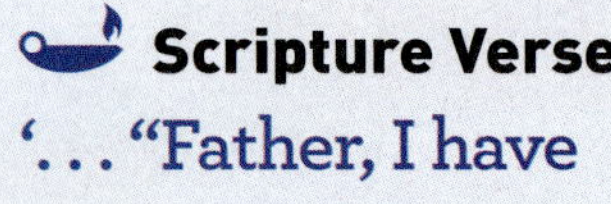

Scripture Verse

'. . . "Father, I have sinned against heaven and against you." '

Luke 15:18

Hear and Believe **Scripture**

The Forgiving Father

Once there was a man who had two sons. The younger son said, "Give me the share of money that should come to me." So his father gave him the money.

The son moved far away. Soon, he spent all of the money! He was hungry and had no place to live.

The son was sorry for the wrong choices he had made. He had wasted the money and hurt his father. The son made up his mind to go home. He would ask his father to forgive him.

While the son was still far from home, his father saw him. He loved his son. The father ran to greet his son. "I am sorry," the son said, "and I am not good enough to be your son." But his father forgave him and he hugged his son. Then he gave his son a big party to celebrate. The son was lost but has been found.

Based on Luke 15:11–24

Knowing Right from Wrong

God lets us choose what to do. We call this **free will**. The boy in the story knew he had done wrong. His **conscience** helped him to know the difference between right and wrong.

Our Church Teaches

We **sin** when we choose to do hurtful things on purpose. When we sin, we hurt our friendship with God and with other people. God wants us to be sorry for our sins. God loves us very much. When we sin, he is ready to show us mercy. God is ready to forgive us.

We Believe

God gives everybody a conscience. God wants us to choose good and stay away from what is evil.

Faith Words

conscience
Our conscience is our ability to know right from wrong.

sin
To sin is to choose to do hurtful things on purpose. Sin is disobeying God.

What are some ways we can practice making good choices?

Saint Paula Frassinetti

Paula was born in Italy in 1809. When she was nine years old, her mother died. Paula had to help take care of her four brothers. Instead of being angry and mean to them, Paula took good care of them. She loved them.

Because of her household chores, Paula was unable to go to school. Her brothers shared with her what they learned in school. Paula made the choice to be cheerful. She went to Mass daily and prayed while she worked.

When Paula grew up she opened a school for poor girls. She later founded a religious order to educate poor children.

Today we honor her as Saint Paula. Her feast day is June 11.

What good choices did Saint Paula make?

What good choice did Saint Paula's brothers make?

ACTIVITY

We can practice choosing to do what is right every day. Unscramble the letters to complete the sentence for each picture.

t h g i f

Joey chooses not to

r h a s e

Tonya is happy to

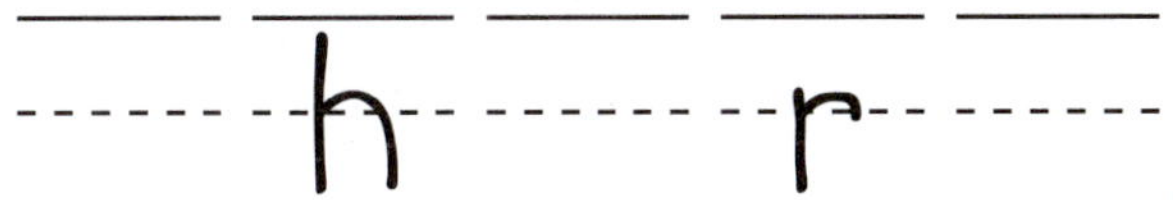

t r t u h

Lily decides to tell the

In what ways can we thank God for the gift of free will?

A Prayer of Action

Making good choices is a type of prayer. When we act in good ways, we praise God. We thank God for the gift of free will. Celebrate making good choices. Pray this prayer together.

Creator God,

thank you for the gift of free will.

Help us to avoid evil and to choose what is good.

Help us to *(add own action)*.

Amen.

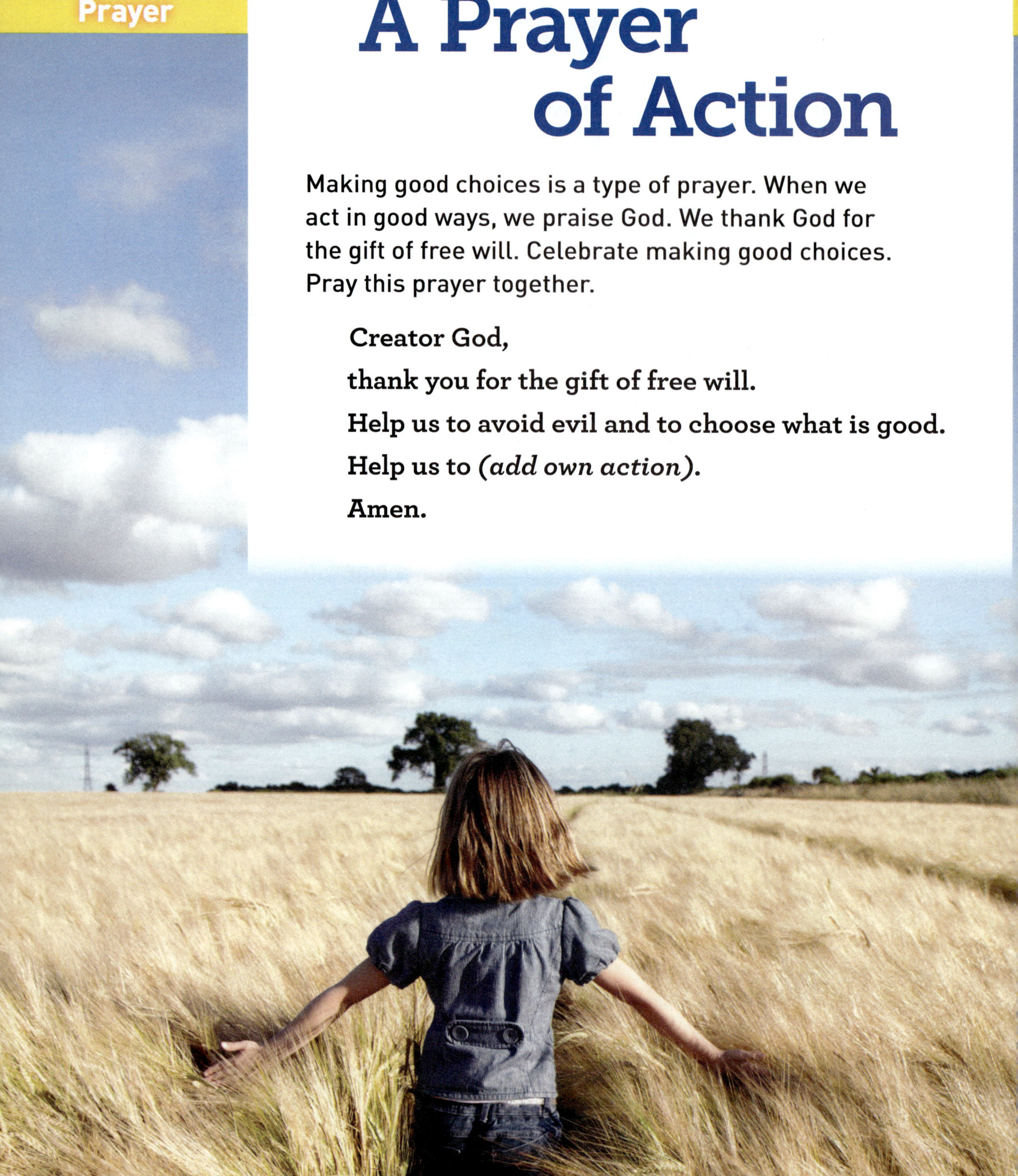

Chapter Review 5

A **Circle** the words that best complete the sentences.

1. God gives us a ______ to help us know right from wrong.

   conscience **free will** **sin**

2. When we do hurtful things on purpose, we ______.

   forgive **love** **sin**

3. God lets us choose what to do. We call this ______.

   conscience **free will** **sin**

4. God wants us to be ______ for our sins.

   angry **happy** **sorry**

B **Draw a line** to connect the parts of each sentence.

1. The son who left home knew •	• **disobeying God.**
2. Before the son said, "I'm sorry," •	• **he had done wrong.**
3. Sin is •	• **his father had forgiven him.**

Faith in Action

Parish Council Members of a parish council help the pastor make choices for the parish. They might help the pastor plan programs. They might help him decide how to improve the church building. The pastor and the parish council try to make good choices.

In Everyday Life

ACTIVITY Some families meet together to make choices. They listen to the needs of one another. Talk about ways family meetings can be helpful. Then draw a picture of your family members meeting together.

In Your Parish

ACTIVITY One parish has chosen how to spend its money. Find its choices.

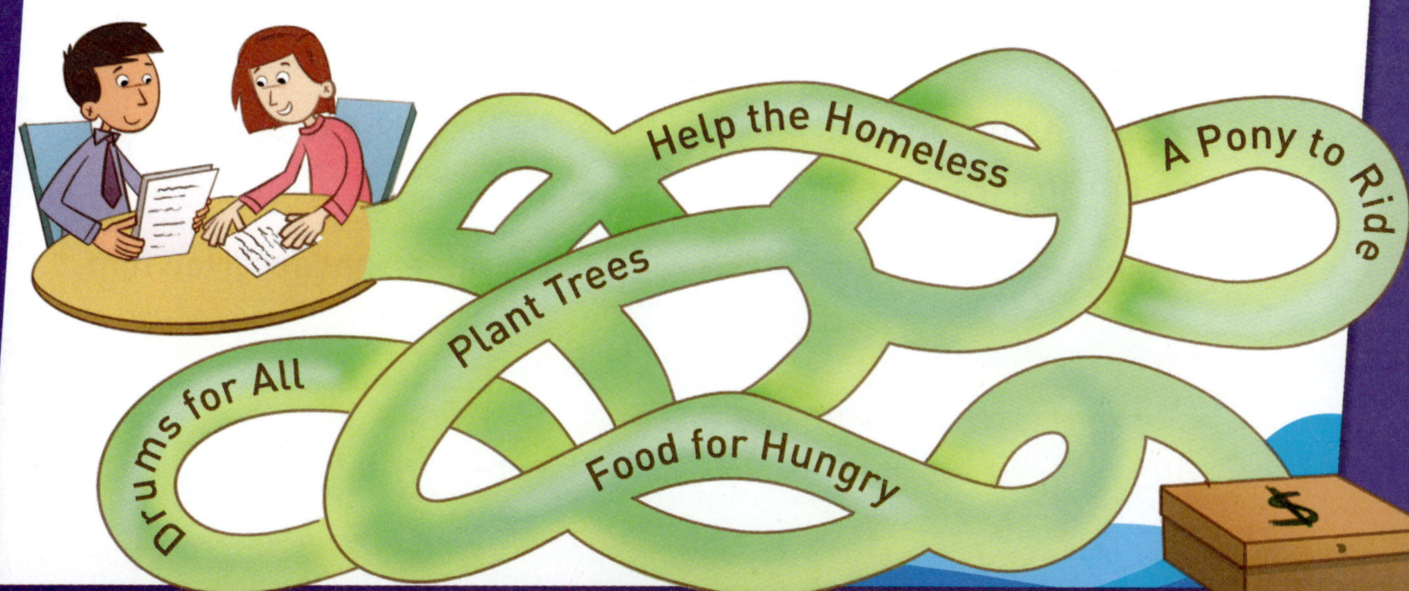

Take Home

Celebrate God's Forgiveness

One of the great joys of Christian life is that we can always trust in God's mercy. Even though we turn away from God when we sin, God never turns away from us. He is always ready to welcome us back.

ACTIVITY **Pretzels and Prayer**

Thaw some frozen bread dough. Break off small pieces and roll them into ropes. Form loops. Bring the ends of the loops up and cross them. Sprinkle salt on the pretzels and bake them. Share with your child that the pretzel shape represents an attitude of prayer, with arms crossed.

THROUGH THE WEEK

A PRAYER FOR THE WEEK I'm sorry, Lord, for the things I have done to hurt others. Help me forgive others when they hurt me. Merciful God, I trust in your love and forgiveness. Amen.

ON SUNDAY
During the prayer before Communion, "Lord, I am not worthy. . . ," remember that God is always ready to forgive.

ON THE WEB
BlestAreWe.com
RCLBLectionary.com
SaintsResource.com

Saint Edith Stein (1891–1942)

Edith Stein converted from Judaism to Catholicism and became a Carmelite nun. She was captured by the Nazis and taken to Auschwitz, where she helped others until her death. She was canonized in 1998.

Patron Saint of:
World Youth Day

Feast Day: August 9

Take Home

Scripture Background
In the Time of the Early Church

Reconciliation Reconciliation most often refers to the new relationship between God and humanity brought about by Christ's redemptive acts. Through Christ's Death on the Cross, humanity achieves peace with God. In many of Paul's letters, the idea of reconciliation goes beyond God and the individual to include the reconciliation of Jews and Gentiles. Paul further describes a need for reconciliation of the world with God.

You can read a description of reconciliation in Romans 5:8–11.

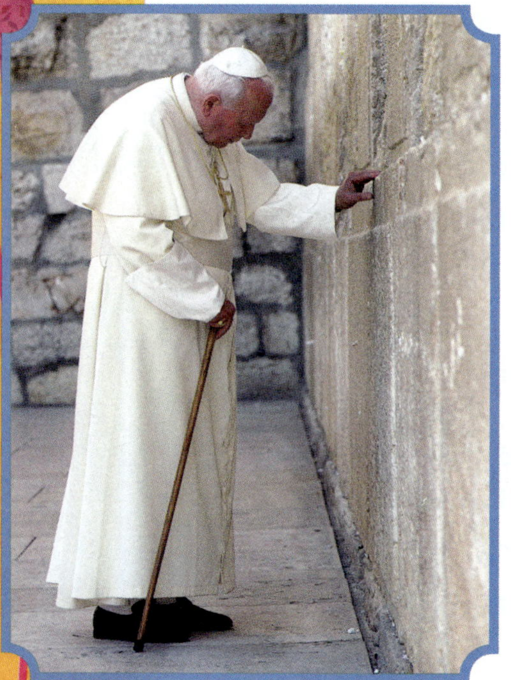

Pope John Paul II at the Western Wall

Our Catholic Tradition
in Interfaith Relations

Jewish-Catholic Relations While he served as pope, Saint John Paul II apologized to the Jewish people for the prejudice some Catholics have shown them throughout history. He asked the Jews for forgiveness. The pope was speaking as the head of the Catholic Church, in the name of all of its members, when he apologized for all the injustices inflicted upon the Jews by any Catholic people. It was an important move toward reconciliation between two peoples who worship the one true God.

Celebrate God's Forgiveness

Chapter 6

Lord, you are good and forgiving, . . . Psalm 86:5

Share

Sometimes we say or do things that hurt other people. We can lose their friendship.

ACTIVITY

Put the pictures in order.
Write 1, 2, 3, and 4 in the boxes.
Then read the story about losing a friend and then making up.

In what ways can we receive God's forgiveness?

Making Up

The **Sacrament of Penance and Reconciliation** celebrates the gift of God's forgiveness. Follow Michael through his celebration of the Sacrament.

Welcome Father Lee greets Michael. Together they make the Sign of the Cross.

Reading Father reads from the Bible. Michael hears about God's love and forgiveness.

Confession Michael talks about, or confesses, his sins. He knows Father Lee cannot tell anyone what he says in confession. He asks Michael to say a prayer or do a kind act. This will make up for what he has done wrong. This prayer or action is called a **penance**.

Prayer of Sorrow Michael says a prayer of sorrow called the Act of Contrition. He tells God he is sorry. He will try not to sin again.

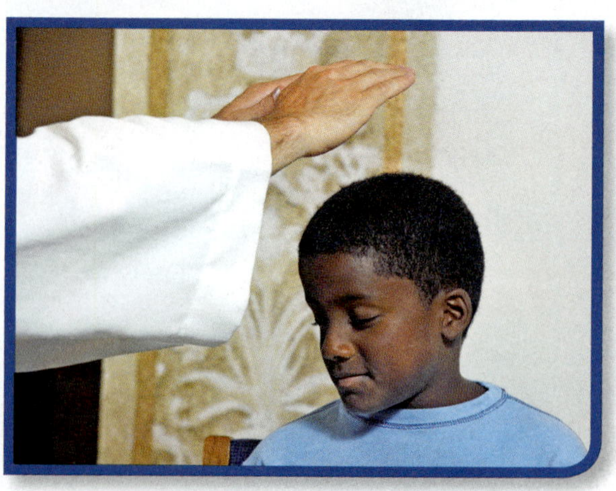

Absolution Father Lee asks God to forgive Michael. He gives Michael **absolution** in the name of the Father, Son, and Holy Spirit. Absolution is God's forgiveness, given through the priest. Then Father Lee gives thanks and says, "Go in peace." Michael answers, "Amen."

A Sacrament of Healing

When we have sinned, we need to say we are sorry. We need to ask for forgiveness. In the Sacrament of Penance and Reconciliation, God heals us by forgiving our sins. God brings us peace.

Our Church Teaches

The Sacrament of Penance and Reconciliation helps us make peace with God and the Catholic Church. The gift of God's **grace** helps us stay away from sin. Grace is the gift of God's life within us that fills us with his love.

ACTIVITY

Color in the boxes with K, Q, or X to find eight words that are part of the Sacrament of Penance and Reconciliation.

P	C	O	N	T	R	I	T	I	O	N
E	K	K	X	W	X	X	K	X	C	Q
N	Q	X	X	E	Q	Q	X	Q	O	X
A	B	S	O	L	U	T	I	O	N	B
N	K	X	Q	C	Q	X	X	K	F	I
C	Q	Q	F	O	R	G	I	V	E	B
E	K	X	X	M	X	Q	Q	K	S	L
X	P	R	I	E	S	T	Q	X	S	E

GO TO Go to page 16 and pray the Act of Contrition.

We Believe

In the Sacrament of Penance and Reconciliation, we celebrate God's love, peace, and forgiveness.

Faith Words

Sacrament of Penance and Reconciliation
Penance and Reconciliation is a Sacrament of Healing that celebrates God's love and forgiveness.

absolution
Absolution is God's forgiveness given through the priest in the Sacrament of Penance and Reconciliation.

In what ways can we practice being people who forgive?

Respond

A Time to Ask for Forgiveness

Drew and Mark's father built them a tree house. It was a great tree house! Drew wanted to play in it with his friends. He did not want his little brother Mark with them.

One day, Mark just could not wait any longer for his turn. So he climbed up the ladder. "It's my turn now," he said.

Drew pushed Mark down. Mark broke his arm. He had to wear a cast for a long time. Drew was sorry that he had pushed Mark. He did not mean to hurt him.

How could Drew make up with Mark?

ACTIVITIES

1. Complete the sentences with these forgiveness words.

sorry　　forgive　　make up

Drew and Mark should ______________________.

Drew should say to Mark, "I am ______________________."

Mark should say to Drew, "I ______________________ you."

2. Put the parts of the Sacrament of Penance and Reconciliation in order. Write the numbers 1, 2, 3, and 4 in the boxes.

☐ pray a prayer of sorrow　　☐ be given a penance

☐ receive absolution　　☐ confess sins

How can we ask for God's forgiveness?

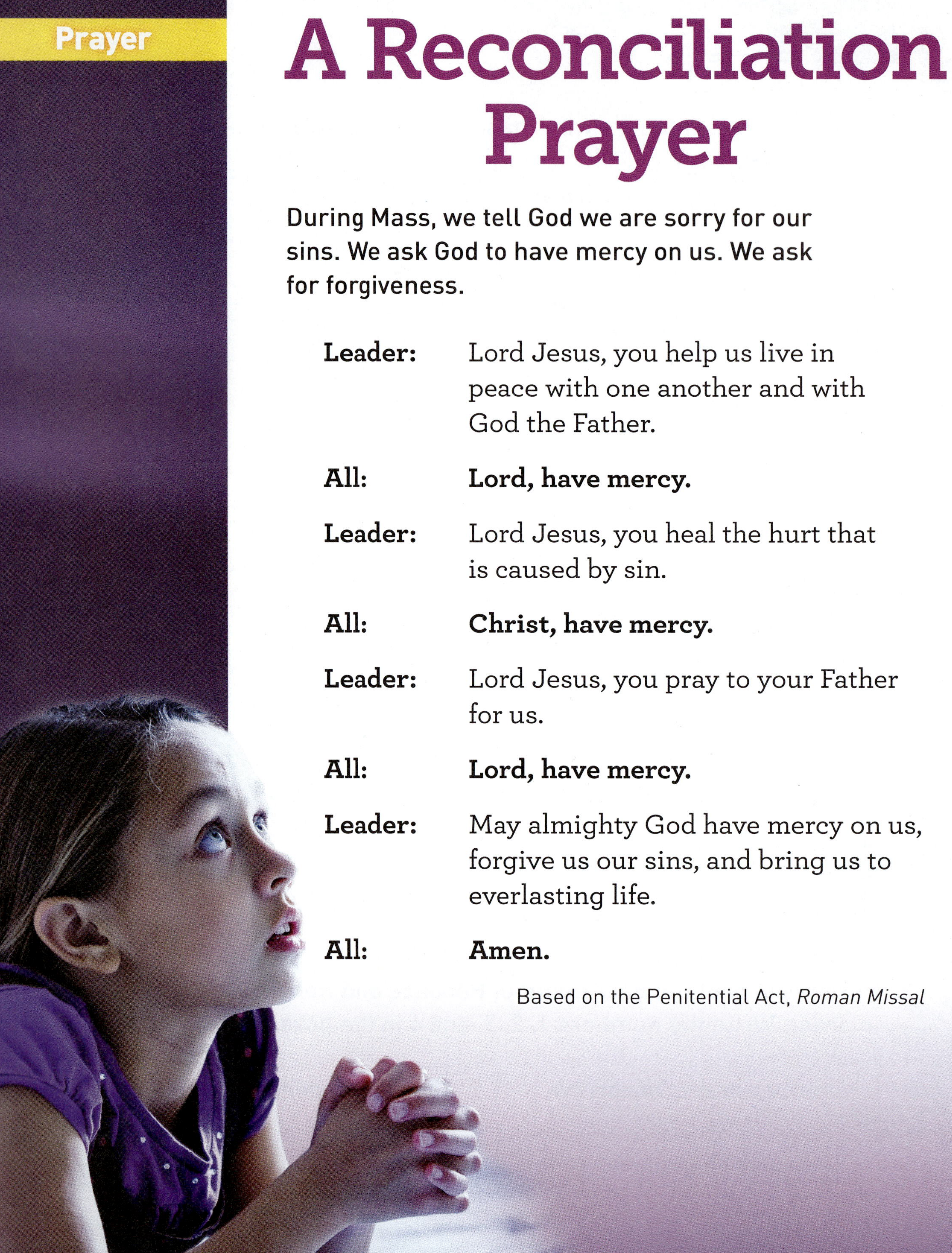

Prayer

A Reconciliation Prayer

During Mass, we tell God we are sorry for our sins. We ask God to have mercy on us. We ask for forgiveness.

Leader: Lord Jesus, you help us live in peace with one another and with God the Father.

All: **Lord, have mercy.**

Leader: Lord Jesus, you heal the hurt that is caused by sin.

All: **Christ, have mercy.**

Leader: Lord Jesus, you pray to your Father for us.

All: **Lord, have mercy.**

Leader: May almighty God have mercy on us, forgive us our sins, and bring us to everlasting life.

All: **Amen.**

Based on the Penitential Act, *Roman Missal*

Chapter Review 6

A **Complete** each sentence. Draw a line to the correct word.

1. In Penance and Reconciliation, we ______ our sins to a priest.	**absolution**
2. ______ is a Sacrament of Healing that celebrates God's love and forgiveness.	**confess**
3. God's forgiveness, given through the priest is ______.	**grace**
4. The gift of God's life within us that fills us with his love is ______.	**Penance and Reconciliation**

B **Write** your own prayer asking forgiveness from God.

Faith in Action

A Parish Priest A parish priest serves the parish and school in many ways. He preaches at Mass. The priest acts in the Person of Christ to forgive sins in the Sacrament of Penance and Reconciliation. Jesus himself gave priests this power on the day of his Resurrection. A priest visits children in the hospital. Children enjoy stories the priest tells about Jesus.

In Everyday Life

ACTIVITY The priest does many things for the community. What are some ways we can help him in his ministry?

____

____

____

____

____

____

In Your Parish

ACTIVITY Put an **X** in the box to show where you think a priest would do each activity.

	In Church	Not In Church
ride a bike		
baptize a baby		
celebrate Mass		
eat pizza		
play baseball		
listen to someone's confession		

Getting ready for Chapter 7

Take Home

We Think About Our Choices

This chapter deals with making choices and presents the Ten Commandments as guides by which we measure our choices. Choices that do not obey God's Commandments are sins. The children will consider the differences between mistakes, venial sins, and mortal sins.

ACTIVITY **Choose a Game**

Choose and play together a board game that involves choices. This will help demonstrate how the choices we make lead to consequences.

THROUGH THE WEEK

A PRAYER FOR THE WEEK Jesus, help us to follow the example of Saint Andrew by placing our trust in you. Help us to take responsibility for our actions. Amen.

ON SUNDAY
Talk with your family about ways to honor the Lord's Day, such as going to Mass, avoiding conflict, and thinking about what God wants you to do.

ON THE WEB
BlestAreWe.com
RCLBLectionary.com
SaintsResource.com

Saint Andrew the Apostle (first century)

Andrew and his brother, Peter, fished for a living in the Sea of Galilee. A disciple of John the Baptist, Andrew was the first Apostle called by Jesus. He then brought Peter to Jesus.

Patron Saint of:
Russia and Scotland

Feast Day: November 30

Take Home

Scripture Background
Before the Time of Jesus

Mount Sinai Mount Sinai is part of the mountain range of Mount Horeb. The Israelites believed that God dwelt on Sinai because Moses received the Ten Commandments from God there. During the Exodus from Egypt, the Israelites lived at the base of the mountain. In Galatians 4:21–27, Paul compares Mount Sinai to the heavenly Jerusalem, to show Jesus' fulfillment of the redemptive promise.

For an account of Moses' experience, read Exodus 20:1–17.

Logo for Jubilee Year of Mercy 2015–2016

Our Catholic Tradition in Jubilee Years

Jubilee Year of Mercy A jubilee year is a special year celebrated by the Church and is a year of remission or forgiveness of sins and universal pardon. In 2015, Pope Francis called for a Jubilee Year of Mercy that began on the Solemnity of the Immaculate Conception (December 8, 2015) and concluded on the Solemnity of Our Lord Jesus Christ, King of the Universe (November 20, 2016). He said, "[T]his is a time for mercy. It is the favorable time to heal wounds, . . . a time to offer everyone, everyone, the way of forgiveness and reconciliation."

Learn more about jubilee years at usccb.org.

We Think About Our Choices

Chapter 7

Make known to me your ways, LORD;
teach me your paths. Psalm 25:4

Share

As we grow up, we learn to be responsible for our actions. We are responsible when we do our work. We are responsible when we take good care of things.

ACTIVITY

Check (✓) each sentence that tells how you can be a responsible person.

- [ ] 1. I feed the family pet.
- [ ] 2. I help Mom and Dad.
- [ ] 3. I do my homework.
- [ ] 4. I listen to my teacher.
- [ ] 5. I lose my library books.
- [ ] 6. I hang up my jacket.

Name other ways to show that you are responsible.

What is one way we can be responsible Church members?

Hear and Believe **Scripture**

The Ten Commandments

Moses was on a mountaintop when God spoke to him. God wanted to help everyone lead good lives. He gave Moses the laws called the Ten Commandments. These laws call for people to love and respect God and others. After receiving the laws, Moses went down the mountain. He told the Jewish people about these laws of God.

The Ten Commandments remind people to rest and pray on the Lord's Day. They tell people to obey their parents, and to avoid telling lies or stealing. The Commandments also say not to hurt other people nor to be jealous of them.

Based on Exodus 20:1–17

Scripture Verse

I am the LORD your God, . . .

Exodus 20:2

We Follow God's Laws

The Ten Commandments are God's laws. As God's only Son, Jesus understood the laws given by his Father in a special way. He taught them to his followers. They help people know right from wrong.

Our Church Teaches

When we know that something is wrong and we do it anyway, we sin. Sin turns us away from God and other people. A **mortal sin** is the most serious kind of sin. It separates us completely from God's grace. To be a mortal sin, a person must do something that is very wrong. The person must also know that it is wrong and do it anyway. We must go to the Sacrament of Penance and Reconciliation to ask God's forgiveness for a mortal sin. A **venial sin** is a less serious kind of sin. It weakens our love for God and others, but does not take it away.

We Believe

God gave us the Ten Commandments to help us know how to lead good lives.

Faith Words

mortal sin
A mortal sin is the most serious kind of sin. It separates us completely from God's grace.

venial sin
A venial sin is a less serious sin. It weakens our love for God and others.

What do the Ten Commandments help us think about?

Respond

An Examination of Conscience

We prepare to celebrate the Sacrament of Penance and Reconciliation. We think about the Ten Commandments. We think about how well we have followed each one. This is called an examination of conscience.

God's Laws	My Actions
1. I am the LORD your God: you shall not have strange gods before me.	Do I believe in God and love God with all my heart?
2. You shall not take the name of the LORD your God in vain.	Do I use the names of God, Jesus, Mary, and the saints with respect?
3. Remember to keep holy the LORD's day.	Do I participate in Mass on Sunday?
4. Honor your father and your mother.	Do I respect and obey my parents?
5. You shall not kill.	Do I treat all God's creatures with respect?
6. You shall not commit adultery.	Do I take good care of my body and respect the bodies of others?
7. You shall not steal.	Have I taken something that belongs to someone else?
8. You shall not bear false witness against your neighbor.	Do I sometimes lie?
9. You shall not covet your neighbor's wife.	Do I treat other families with respect?
10. You shall not covet your neighbor's goods.	Am I ever jealous or greedy?

Mistakes and sins are not the same. You might break a glass by mistake. You sin when you choose to do something you know is wrong.

ACTIVITY

Follow the stone path. If the stone tells about a mistake, color it yellow. If the stone tells about a sin, color it red.

8. Oops! I spilled milk on my new jacket.

7. I stole my brother's cell phone and played with it.

6. I had a big fight with a friend.

4. I was jealous of my friend's new bike.

5. I left the window open and the rain came in.

3. I left my homework at home.

2. I lost my sweatshirt at school.

1. I lied about how much time I spent playing video games.

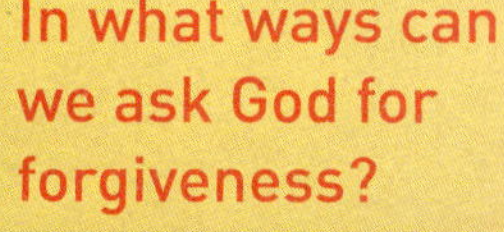

A Prayer for Forgiveness

Leader: God has given us the gift of free will. We use this gift when we choose between good actions and sinful ones. We use it in prayer to ask God to forgive our sins. Let us pray.

Side 1: God our Father, sometimes we have not behaved well.

All: **Forgive us and show us your mercy.**

Side 2: Sometimes we have fought.

All: **Forgive us and show us your mercy.**

Side 1: Sometimes we have been lazy.

All: **Forgive us and show us your mercy.**

Side 2: Sometimes we have told lies.

All: **Forgive us and show us your mercy. Amen.**

Based on *Rite of Penance, Appendix II*, 50

Chapter Review 7

A **Circle** the words that best complete the sentences.

1. Telling a lie is ______.

   responsible **not responsible** **okay**

2. God gave Moses laws called the ______ Commandments.

   Great **Five** **Ten**

3. The Third Commandment tells us to go to ______ on Sunday.

   Mass **meetings** **movies**

4. The Fifth Commandment tells us to ______ all God made.

   disrespect **respect** **use up**

5. Mistakes are ______ and not sins.

   accidents **laws** **plans**

B **Complete** the definitions.

1. A mortal sin is the most serious kind of sin. It
   ____
   ____
   us completely from God's grace.

2. A venial sin is a less serious sin. It
   ____
   ____
   our love for God and others.

Faith in Action

Community Outreach There are many ways for students to serve others. Some children put together Friendship Boxes for the Red Cross to give to homeless children. Some write letters to public officials about the rights people have. Some children go together to visit people living in a nursing home.

In Everyday Life

ACTIVITY In the first column are responsibilities we have. In the second column are the rights that match them. Draw a line to match each responsibility with the right that fits it.

Responsibilities	Rights
1. Abby studies for her test. •	• Food
2. Ben does not waste food at lunch. •	• Family
3. Miguel goes to church with his family. •	• School
4. Hailey does chores around the house. •	• Shelter
5. Emily respects her parents. •	• Religion

In Your Parish

ACTIVITY Think about ways you treat others in your church and at school. Write about a time you stood up for someone who was being treated unfairly.

Getting ready for Chapter 8

Take Home

We Say We Are Sorry

When we choose to do wrong, we need to say we are sorry to God and to any person we have hurt. The focus of this chapter is to learn to use prayer to tell God that we are sorry. Children will learn that prayer brings us closer to God and that with the Holy Spirit's help we can change.

ACTIVITY **Ways to Say "I'm Sorry"**

With your child think of several ways to say or show that you are sorry. Make a list of your ideas, and use them when you need to say, "I'm sorry."

THROUGH THE WEEK

A PRAYER FOR THE WEEK O Lord, may our family be as holy as that of Elizabeth and Zechariah. Help us to recognize wrongs we have done to family members. Strengthen us to admit our faults and to say we are sorry. Amen.

ON SUNDAY
During the Sunday liturgy, ask God's forgiveness for wrong choices you made last week.

ON THE WEB
BlestAreWe.com
RCLBLectionary.com
SaintsResource.com

Saint Elizabeth (first century)

Elizabeth was Mary's cousin. She and Zechariah were the parents of John the Baptist. The angel Gabriel told Zechariah that John would be filled with the Holy Spirit. John's parents trusted God.

Patron Saint of: pregnant women

Feast Day: November 5

Take Home

Scripture Background
In the Time of Jesus

Repentance The Old Testament prophets called people to repent and offered the hope of salvation. Many women of the Bible kept this hope alive—women like Sarah, Rebecca, and Esther. The last of the prophets was John the Baptist, who preached repentance for the forgiveness of sins. He prepared the way for the long-promised Messiah. When Jesus was baptized by John he was revealed as the Anointed One of God and he began his public ministry. Jesus' message was and is to reform our lives and believe in his Good News—that he was ushering in the Kingdom of God and the arrival, through him, of salvation.

You can read of John's call to repentance in Matthew 3:1–17.

Our Catholic Tradition in Music

Fiddler on the Roof *Fiddler on the Roof* tells the story of a Russian Jewish family. One of the most poignant songs, "Sunrise, Sunset," sung by the mother and father, tells how quickly time passes in a family and how quickly children grow up. This song echoes the sentiment of Catholic parents as well. It reminds us that we should nurture our relationships with our children, because they won't be with us forever.

We Say We Are Sorry

Chapter 8

When a sinner is sorry, there is great joy in Heaven.

Based on Luke 15:7

Share

There are many ways to say, "I'm sorry."
You can say it with words like, "Let's make up."
You can say it with an action like a hug.

ACTIVITY

Tell another good way to say, "I'm sorry."

In what way can we tell God we are sorry?

Hear and Believe **Scripture**

Return to God!

John the Baptist was a holy man. He told other people how to find God's forgiveness.

John: Return to God! Repent! God's kingdom is coming!

Woman: What does repent mean?

John: Repent means to be truly sorry for your sins.

Boy: What else does repent mean?

John: It means that you really want to change.

Girl: Is that all we need to do to return to God?

John: No. You must also do penance. Penance is a prayer or an act to make up for the harm caused by sin.

Many people heard John's words. They repented. They told God they were sorry. Then John baptized them in the river.

Based on Matthew 3:1–8

Scripture Verse

. . . 'Prepare the way of the Lord, . . .'

Matthew 3:3

Returning to God

Sin separates us from God. John the Baptist wanted people to return to God. We can return to God by telling him we are sorry for our sins. When we are sorry for our sins, we feel **contrition**. Contrition means being sorry and wanting to do better.

Our Church Teaches

To show that we are sorry for our sins, we pray the **Act of Contrition**. This is a prayer of sorrow. In this prayer we promise to try not to sin again. When we are sorry for our sins, the Holy Spirit helps us do better.

We Believe

When we sin, we can return to God. We tell God we are sorry. We ask the Holy Spirit to guide us. We make up our minds not to sin again.

Faith Words

contrition
Contrition is sorrow for doing wrong and wanting to stay away from sin.

Act of Contrition
The Act of Contrition is a prayer that tells God we are sorry for our sins.

In what ways do we show we are sorry for our sins?

A Penance Service

Matt and Kate went to a penance service. Many other people were there, too. Everyone had come because they wanted to return to God. They listened to a story that Jesus once told. It is about a shepherd and a lost sheep.

A shepherd had one hundred sheep. One sheep got lost. The shepherd went to look for it. When he found the sheep, the shepherd was very happy. In the same way, there is great joy in Heaven when a sinner repents.

Based on Luke 15:4–7

God is like the shepherd in the story. He rejoices when we return to him.

Why is this a good story for a penance service?

Scripture Verse

'Rejoice with me because I have found my lost sheep.'

Luke 15:6

ACTIVITY

Use the secret code to write the missing letters.
Then read the prayer of sorrow.

Secret Code

1	2	3	4	5	6	7	8	9	10	11	12	13
A	B	C	D	E	F	G	H	I	J	K	L	M
14	**15**	**16**	**17**	**18**	**19**	**20**	**21**	**22**	**23**	**24**	**25**	**26**
N	O	P	Q	R	S	T	U	V	W	X	Y	Z

__ __ __ __ __ __, __
6 1 20 8 5 18 9

__ __ __ __ __ __ __
1 13 19 15 18 18 25

__ __ __ __ __ __
6 15 18 1 12 12

__ __ __ __ __ __.
13 25 19 9 14 19

What does it mean to return to God?

Prayer

An Act of Contrition

Leader: When we sin, one way to return to God is to pray a prayer of sorrow. We also think of ways to try to do better.

All: **My God,**
I am sorry for my sins with all my heart.
In choosing to do wrong
and failing to do good,
I have sinned against you
whom I should love above all things.
I firmly intend, with your help,
to do penance,
to sin no more,
and to avoid whatever leads me to sin.
Our Savior Jesus Christ
suffered and died for us.
In his name, my God, have mercy.

Rite of Penance

Leader: God always seeks us out when we walk away from the path of goodness. God is always ready to forgive us when we have sinned.

All: **Amen.**

Chapter Review 8

A **Complete** each sentence by drawing a line to the correct word.

1. ______ means to be sorry and to want to do better.	• Act of Contrition
2. A prayer or act to make up for the harm caused by sin is called a ______.	• Contrition
3. To show that we are sorry, we pray an ______.	• prayer of sorrow

B **Draw or write.** What did Jesus say happens in Heaven when a sinner repents?

Faith in Action

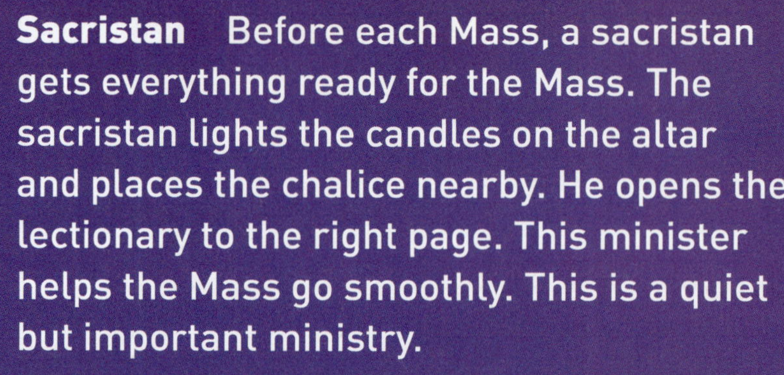

Sacristan Before each Mass, a sacristan gets everything ready for the Mass. The sacristan lights the candles on the altar and places the chalice nearby. He opens the lectionary to the right page. This minister helps the Mass go smoothly. This is a quiet but important ministry.

In Everyday Life

ACTIVITY Every person has a job to do. What is one of your jobs? Think of a time that you failed to do your job. How did your choice affect others? Discuss your answer with a classmate.

In Your Parish

ACTIVITY Get the altar ready for Mass. Draw lines to put items in the right places.

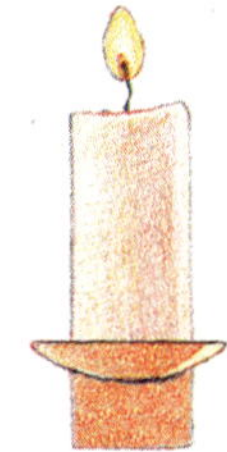

We Celebrate the Word of God

Unit 3

The Gospels tell us the message of Jesus. When we listen to the Scripture readings, we are taught the way of the Gospel. We are inspired to live as true followers of Jesus.

"But some seed fell on rich soil, and produced fruit, a hundred or sixty or thirtyfold. Whoever has ears ought to hear."

Matthew 13:8–9

A farmer plants seeds that will grow into food. Like seeds, our faith grows when we listen to God's Word.

Unit 3 SONG

Go and Listen

Words and Music by Robert J. Batastini

Cantor, All repeat

Go and lis - ten to the Word of God.

Cantor, All repeat

God has the words of ev - er - last - ing life.

© 2003, GIA Publications, Inc.

Getting ready for Chapter 9

Take Home

We Learn About God's Love

The Bible is a book filled with many kinds of literature, such as stories, letters, prayers, and songs. It tells of God's love for us from the moment of creation on. This chapter encourages the children to be aware of the Bible as a tool for learning about God's gift of creation, his love for us, and his gift of his Son, Jesus.

ACTIVITY **Creating with Clay**

According to one account in Genesis, God made us out of clay. Together, use clay to create a symbol of God's love for your family.

THROUGHOUT THE WEEK

A PRAYER FOR THE WEEK O Lord, Saint Angela Merici wanted to share the Word of God with others. Help us to open our hearts to your words in the Bible. Teach us to protect all that you have made. Amen.

ON SUNDAY
Listen to the readings at Mass. Later in the day, choose one of the readings to discuss with your family.

ON THE WEB
BlestAreWe.com
RCLBLectionary.com
SaintsResource.com

Saint Angela Merici (1474–1540)

Angela Merici wanted children and their families to learn to love God. She and her friends started teaching religion classes. They opened a school under the protection of Saint Ursula.

Patron Saint of:
the sick and people with disabilities

Feast Day: January 27

Take Home

Scripture Background
In the Time of Jesus

Birds Because of its varied climates and types of environments, the Holy Land attracts many species of birds. The Bible refers to fifty different species. Over forty books in the Bible mention birds, such as eagles, owls, storks, quails, hens, and sparrows. In Jesus' time, all small birds were called sparrows. Jesus spoke of his Father's concern for all of creation, even small birds. Both Matthew and Luke refer to sparrows in their Gospels.

You can read about attention given to sparrows in Matthew 10:27–33.

Our Catholic Tradition in Art

Illumination The painstaking work of monks and artists of the Middle Ages has left us with some priceless treasures of Scriptures, prayer books, and other writings copied and illuminated by hand. In an illuminated manuscript, the text was supplemented by the addition of decorations, often to the first letter of the text and the borders and miniature illustrations. Artists used bright colors along with gold and silver to intertwine pictures of flowers and animals and to depict scenes from the text. The artworks are extraordinarily detailed and beautiful. They show the monks' and artists' dedication to preserving the written word.

We Learn About God's Love

Chapter 9

The Lord God took Adam and settled him in the garden of Eden to care for it. *Based on* Genesis 2:15

Share

The world that God created has mountains, forests, and deserts. It has rivers, lakes, and oceans.

The earth has many kinds of plants and animals, too. Name some plants and animals you know about.

ACTIVITY

Draw a picture of yourself taking care of something God created.

What does creation tell us about God?

Hear and Believe Scripture

God Loves All Creation

One day, Jesus told his followers this story about God's love.

"Some people worry about what they will eat and drink. Other people worry about what clothes to wear. But I say, do not worry. Instead, look at the birds in the sky. God takes good care of them. Look at the flowers in the field. God takes good care of them too.

"So have faith. God loves you even more than the birds and flowers. He is a loving Father who knows what you need. God will always take care of you."

Based on Matthew 6:25–34

Ways We Learn About God

God is the Creator of all things. In the **Bible** we read that he made all things good. God promises to take care of us. God asks us to take care of **creation**. The story Jesus told about God taking care of all creation is a Bible story. The Bible is called the **Word of God**. Its words tell what God wants us to know about himself. We also call Jesus the Word of God. He shows us most fully who God is.

Our Church Teaches

The Bible is also called **Sacred Scripture**, which means "holy writings." The teachings of Jesus are in the Bible. Jesus is the **Son of God**.

GO TO page 15 to learn more about the Bible.

We Believe

We learn about God's love for us from the Bible. He made all creation good. We are to care for God's creation.

Faith Words

Bible
The Bible is called the Word of God. Its words tell what God wants us to know about himself. We also call Jesus the Word of God. He shows most fully who God is.

Word of God
The Word of God is God speaking to us in the Bible.

Sacred Scripture
The Bible is called Sacred Scripture.

Son of God
Jesus is the Son of God. He is true God and true man.

In what ways can people show love for God's creation?

Respond Caring for God's Creation

Where there had once been an empty lot there is now a community garden. Anna's family and other neighbors cleaned up the lot. They broke up the hard soil. Now they grow flowers, fruits, and vegetables there. They even recycle things to use in their garden. These neighbors are showing respect for the earth.

How can you care for God's creation?

ACTIVITIES

1. Learn to sign the words "God cares for you."

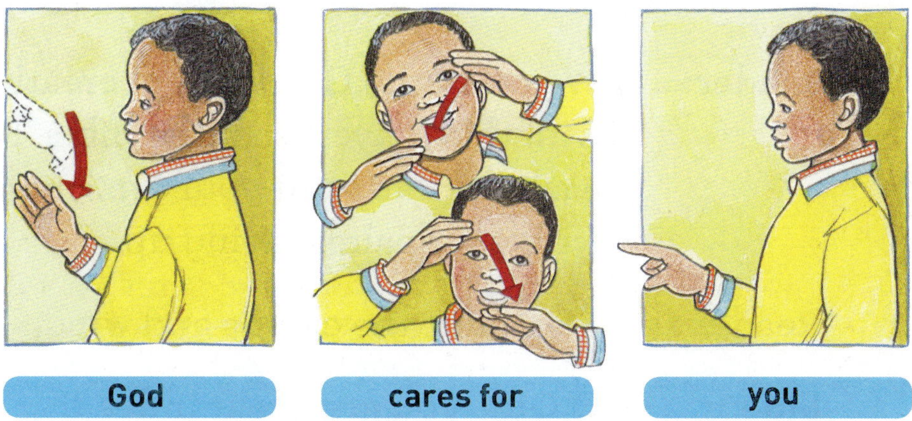

2. See the word CREATION below. Think of something God made that begins with each letter. Write the words on the lines. The first one is done for you.

In what ways can the Bible help us celebrate God's love?

A Psalm About Creation

Scripture Verse

Give thanks to him,
bless his name; . . .

Psalm 100:4

Leader:	We celebrate God's gift of creation with this prayer from the Bible. For each response, lift your arms high with your palms facing up.
Reader 1:	You made the clouds and wind.
Side 1:	**O God, you are great indeed!**
Reader 2:	You made the land and seas.
Side 2:	**O God, your works are wonderful!**
Reader 3:	You made the sun and moon.
Side 1:	**O God, you are great indeed!**
Reader 4:	You made lakes and mountains.
Side 2:	**O God, your works are wonderful!**
Reader 5:	You made the trees and birds.
Side 1:	**O God, you are great indeed!**
Leader:	How can we celebrate God's love?
All:	**We will sing praise to God.**

Based on Psalm 104

Chapter Review 9

A **List** five things that the Bible tells us God created.

B **Write** the letter for the missing word in each sentence.

A Bible	B care	C creation	D Son	E worry

1. We learn about God's love for us from the ☐.
2. God takes care of all ☐.
3. Jesus tells us not to ☐.
4. Jesus is the ☐ of God .
5. God will always take ☐ of us.

Faith in Action

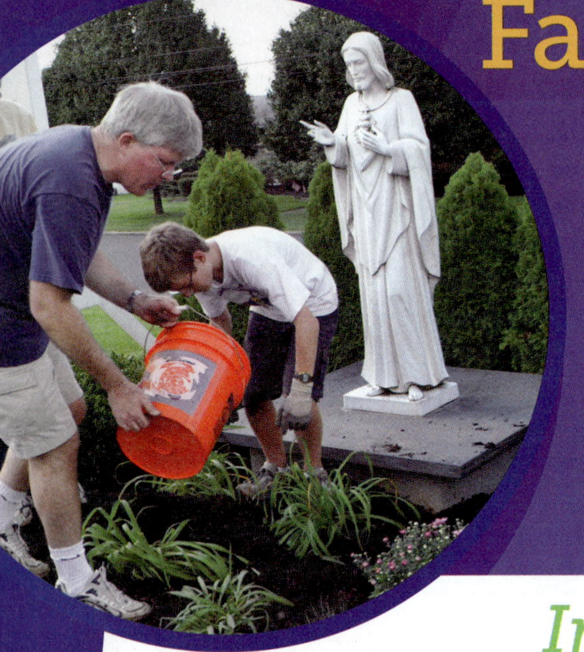

Green Thumbs Committee Senior citizens and young people work together on this committee. The older people are good at growing plants and trees. The young people help them. Together they care for God's creation.

In Your Parish

ACTIVITY Think about ways your parish or school uses the gift of water. How does your parish or school show respect for this gift?

In Everyday Life

ACTIVITY Put a ✓ for things you already do for the Earth. Put an ✗ for things you should not do. Put a • for things you will do.

Actions	Do Now	Not Do	Will Do
Recycle paper and plastic.			
Throw empty cans on the grass.			
Plant vegetables and flowers.			
Leave trash on the floor.			
Take care of pets.			

Take Home

We Listen to God's Word

In this chapter, the children will come to realize that when we hear the Scripture readings, we are listening to God's Word. They will learn the responses said during the Liturgy of the Word. They will also learn that the Nicene Creed is a prayer that states the beliefs that Catholics hold.

ACTIVITY **Good News**

Put a "Remember the Good News" sign on your refrigerator to help your family remember to share good news with each other this week. This will prepare your child to learn about the Good News of the Gospels.

THROUGH THE WEEK

A PRAYER FOR THE WEEK Lord, open our ears to hear your Word. Give us the gift of understanding so that we may learn the meaning of your Word for our lives. Amen.

ON SUNDAY
Show your child the Old and New Testaments in the Bible. Point out that the New Testament contains the Gospel stories that tell about Jesus.

ON THE WEB
BlestAreWe.com
RCLBLectionary.com
SaintsResource.com

Saint Hilary of Poitiers (315–368)

Hilary of Poitiers was married and a father before he began to believe in God. As a result of reading the New Testament, he converted to Christianity. He was so greatly respected for his faith and learning that he was later named a bishop.

Patron Saint of:
children with disabilities

Feast Day: January 13

Take Home

Scripture Background
In the Time of Jesus

Crops The most important crops in the Holy Land were barley and wheat, because they formed the basis for bread and were food for animals. Seed was usually sown after the autumn rains. Following winter rains and those of March and April, the barley was ready to be harvested. Wheat was harvested during the summer. After the sheaves were laid out, animals walked on them, which separated the stalks, the chaff, and the grain.

Read the parable of the Sower in Matthew 13:1–9, 18–23.

Our Catholic Tradition in
Church Design

Pulpits Catholic churches usually have a crucifix, statues, a baptismal font, an altar, and an ambo. The ambo reminds us that God speaks to us. Starting around the ninth century, churches had two stands called *ambos*. One was for the Gospel readings and one was for readings from the Epistles. The one for the Gospel readings became more and more ornate until, by the thirteenth century, it became known as the pulpit. The word *pulpit* comes from the Latin *pulpitum*, meaning "stage." These ornate pulpits were at first built in Italian churches. Over time, they have been made in many styles and in many materials such as stone and iron.

We Listen to God's Word

Chapter 10

"Everyone who listens to these words of mine and acts on them will be like a wise man who built his house on rock."

Matthew 7:24

Share

Most people like hearing a good story. To enjoy a story, we need to be good listeners. Good stories can be funny, sad, or even scary. Answer these questions about stories.

ACTIVITY

1. Who is the best storyteller you know?

____

2. What story do you like to listen to again and again?

____

3. Why do you like this story?

____

____

When do Church members listen to the stories of Jesus?

Hear and Believe **Worship**

 A Story About Listening

One day, Jesus told this story about listening to the Word of God.

"A farmer scattered seeds in his field. Some seeds fell on a path. Birds ate them up. Some fell on rocks. They dried up and died. Some seeds fell among thorns. The thorns grew and choked the seeds. Other seeds fell on good soil. They took root, grew, and produced good fruit.

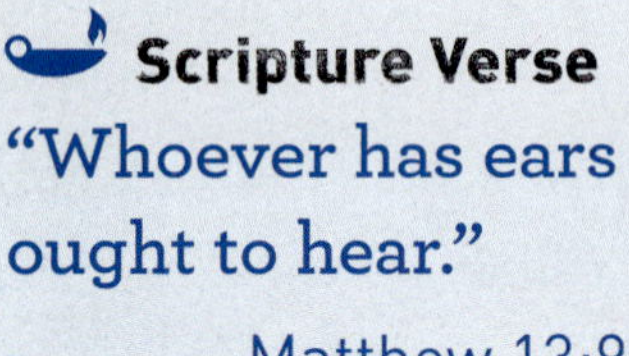

Scripture Verse

"Whoever has ears ought to hear."

Matthew 13:9

"People are like the places where the farmer's seeds fell. People who do not try to understand God's Word are like the path. Some hear God's Word but remember it only a short time. They are like the rocks. Some people hear God's Word. But they let other worries crowd it out. They are like the soil with thorns. Other people hear God's Word and really listen to it. They are like the good soil. Faith grows in them."

Based on Matthew 13:1–9,18–23

Listening to God's Word

This Bible story tells what happens when we really listen to God's Word. Our faith grows. At Mass we listen to God's Word from the Bible.

Our Church Teaches

During the **Liturgy of the Word** on Sunday, we listen to three Bible readings. The first one is from the Old Testament. During the Easter Season, it is taken from the Acts of the Apostles. The second and third readings are from the New Testament. The third reading is also called the Gospel. It tells the story of Jesus's life. After the Gospel, the priest or deacon gives a talk called a **homily**. The homily helps us understand the Bible readings we just heard, our faith, or the feast we are celebrating. Then we all pray the **Nicene Creed**. This prayer says what Catholics believe.

GO TO page 13 to pray the Nicene Creed.

We Believe

At Mass we listen to God's Word. We pray the Nicene Creed to say what we believe.

Faith Words

Liturgy of the Word
The Liturgy of the Word is when we listen to God's Word from the Bible at Mass.

homily
The homily helps us understand the Bible readings we just heard, our faith, or the feast we are celebrating.

Nicene Creed
The Nicene Creed tells the important beliefs of the Catholic faith.

What are some ways we listen during the Liturgy of the Word?

Respond We Take Part at Mass

On Sundays, Anna takes part at Mass with the parish community. She joins others in singing and saying the prayers aloud. Anna also likes hearing Bible stories about God and Jesus. She knows the responses to the Bible readings.

After the First and Second Readings, the lector says, "The word of the Lord."

Anna and others answer, "Thanks be to God."

Everyone stands for the Gospel. After the reading, the priest or deacon says, "The Gospel of the Lord."

Anna knows to answer, "Praise to you, Lord Jesus Christ."

Then Anna sits quietly and listens to the homily. She wants to learn how to be like Jesus.

ACTIVITY

Fill in the missing word in each sentence.

Praise	Word	Gospel	homily	Creed	Thanks

1. We listen to three Bible readings during the Liturgy of the ____________.

2. After the First and Second Readings we say, "____________ be to God."

3. The ____________ tells the story of Jesus' life.

4. After the Gospel we say, "____________ to you, Lord Jesus Christ."

5. The talk given by the priest or deacon is called the ____________.

6. The Nicene ____________ is a prayer that tells what we believe as Catholics.

When in the Mass do we sing our prayer to God?

Prayer

A Responsorial Psalm

Leader: After the First Reading at Mass, we respond with a special sung prayer from the Book of Psalms. It is called the Responsorial Psalm. Let us together pray this Responsorial Psalm about creation.

Reader 1: The seed that falls on good ground will yield a fruitful harvest.

All: **The seed that falls on good ground will yield a fruitful harvest.**

Reader 2: Our God, you take care of the earth and send rain to help the soil grow all kinds of crops.

All: **The seed that falls on good ground will yield a fruitful harvest.**

Reader 3: Your rivers never run dry, and you prepare the earth to produce much grain.

All: **The seed that falls on good ground will yield a fruitful harvest.**

Based on Psalm 65
Lectionary for Masses with Children

Chapter Review 10

A **Draw a line** to connect the parts of each sentence.

1. People who listen to God's Word are like ______ that seeds fall on.	Word
2. At Mass we come together to listen to God's Word from the ______.	Nicene Creed
3. We call this part of Mass the Liturgy of the ______.	good soil
4. Our ______ grows when we really listen to God's Word.	Bible
5. We state what we believe in a prayer called the ______.	faith

B **Number** the parts of the Liturgy of the Word in order.

______ The priest explains the Gospel reading.

______ We listen to an Old Testament reading.

______ We listen to a New Testament reading.

______ We pray the Nicene Creed.

______ We listen to the Gospel.

______ We sing the Responsorial Psalm.

Faith in *Action*

Lectors People who read Scripture to the community at Mass are called lectors. They practice reading God's Word out loud before Mass. They read carefully so everyone can understand the Scripture stories.

In Everyday Life

ACTIVITY Draw a picture of a Gospel story you have heard at Mass. What is the meaning of the story for second-graders?

In Your Parish

ACTIVITY Think about the difference between reading a story and hearing one. What is easier—listening to the story or reading the story? Circle the picture that shows what you find easiest. Be prepared to share why you chose the picture.

Getting ready for Chapter 11

Take Home

We Act on God's Word

Jesus made the treatment of other human beings the focus of his time on Earth. The children will learn that Jesus cared for others to show his love for God. He wants us to do the same by helping and serving others.

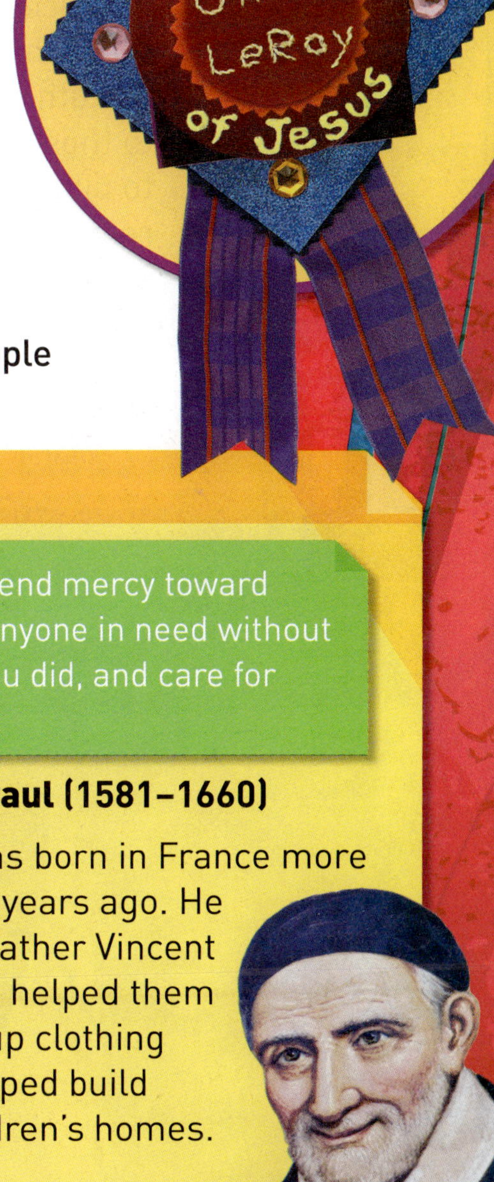

ACTIVITY **Followers of Jesus**

Think of people who showed love for others, such as Saint Teresa of Calcutta and Dr. Martin Luther King, Jr. With your child, make one or more badges to honor people you know who follow Jesus.

THROUGH THE WEEK

A PRAYER FOR THE WEEK Dear Jesus, help us to extend mercy toward others, like Saint Vincent de Paul. Let us not pass by anyone in need without stopping to help. Help us to trust as you did, love as you did, and care for others as you did. Amen.

ON SUNDAY
What do this Sunday's readings tell you about being a good person? Pick one message from the homily to take home from this week's liturgy.

ON THE WEB
BlestAreWe.com
RCLBLectionary.com
SaintsResource.com

Saint Vincent de Paul (1581–1660)

Vincent de Paul was born in France more than four hundred years ago. He became a priest. Father Vincent fed hungry people, helped them find jobs, and set up clothing collections. He helped build hospitals and children's homes.

Patron Saint of:
charitable societies

Feast Day: September 27

Take Home

Scripture Background
In the Time of Jesus

Poverty Poverty in the Holy Land was recognized as the result of social factors, such as injustice, rather than a consequence of personal failings. The practice of leaving grain in the fields for those in need after harvesting is described in Ruth 2:2–9. Responsibility for ministering to those who are poor remains fundamental to biblical faith. Jesus himself speaks of the responsibility to help the poor.

You can read of Jesus' approach to poverty and other issues of justice in Matthew 6:1–4 and 19:21–26.

Our Catholic Tradition
in Literature

The Seven Storey Mountain

Thomas Merton was a Catholic Trappist monk who died in 1968. He converted to Catholicism as a young adult. In 1948 he wrote an autobiography about how he moved from atheism to Catholicism. That book, *The Seven Storey Mountain*, became the most famous memoir ever written by an American Catholic. Merton was a social activist and spoke out on such topics as racial justice, violence, and world peace. His clear vision of how to live a Christian life, his wonderful writing, and his ever-questioning spirit are inspirations for those who have come after him.

We Act on God's Word

Chapter 11

"Amen, amen, I say to you, whoever believes in me will do the works that I do, and will do greater ones than these, . . ." John 14:12

Share

So many actions
that we take.

We walk and ride.
We bake a cake.

So many actions
every day.

We laugh and smile.
We learn and pray.

ACTIVITY

Imagine yourself in each picture. What would you do? Write about an action you would take.

I would

____

______________________________________.

I would

____

______________________________________.

In what ways can we act on God's Word?

Hear and Believe **Scripture**

How Christians Act

Jesus told his followers, "I will return to Earth at the end of time. Then I will judge all the people in the world. I will put the people in two groups. To the first group I will say, 'You have done well. I invite you to stay with me forever.' But I will tell the second group, 'Go away. You have chosen not to be with me forever.'"

Jesus said that the first group had treated everyone as they would have treated him. They gave food to the hungry. They gave drink to people who were thirsty. They made new people feel at home. They shared their own clothes with people who needed them. They cared for the sick. And they visited people in prison.

The first group of people acted on God's Word. Jesus will welcome them to be with him forever.

Based on Matthew 25:31–46

Responding in Action

Jesus showed his followers how to live God's Word. He taught people by his words and actions. We show our love for God by how we treat others.

Our Church Teaches

Jesus told his followers to take care of the needs of others. These actions are called **Works of Mercy**. When we help others in loving **service**, we act as Jesus did.

The Works of Mercy

Feed the hungry.

Give drink to the thirsty.

Shelter the homeless.

Give clothing to the poor.

Visit the sick.

Visit those in prison.

Pray for those who have died.

We Believe

Jesus shows us how to act on God's Word. He teaches us that by loving our neighbor, we show our love for God.

Faith Words

Works of Mercy
The Works of Mercy tell how to take care of the needs of others.

service
Service means doing work that helps others.

In what ways can we act like Jesus?

Respond Saint Martin de Porres

Saint Martin lived a long time ago in Peru, South America. He wanted to spend his life acting on God's Word. So he became a religious brother who worked for the Church. No job was too big for Brother Martin. And no job was too small. He served God in everything he did.

What did Brother Martin do? Sometimes he took food and medicine to the sick. He helped find homes for homeless children. Brother Martin was kind to people no one else loved.

"Why do you do these things?" someone once asked.

"I see the face of Jesus in everyone," Brother Martin said. "When I show love to people, I am showing love to Jesus."

The feast day of Saint Martin de Porres is November 3.

What does Saint Martin's story tell us about loving others?

ACTIVITY

Follow the directions on the path.

Write one way that Saint Martin acted as Jesus did.

Draw a picture about a time that you acted as Jesus did.

Circle one of these Works of Mercy that you have done in the past.

Visit the sick.

Pray for the dead.

Feed the hungry.

Clothe the poor.

Choose another Work of Mercy from page 134 that you will do this week.

Write it on the sign below.

In what way can we celebrate acting on God's Word?

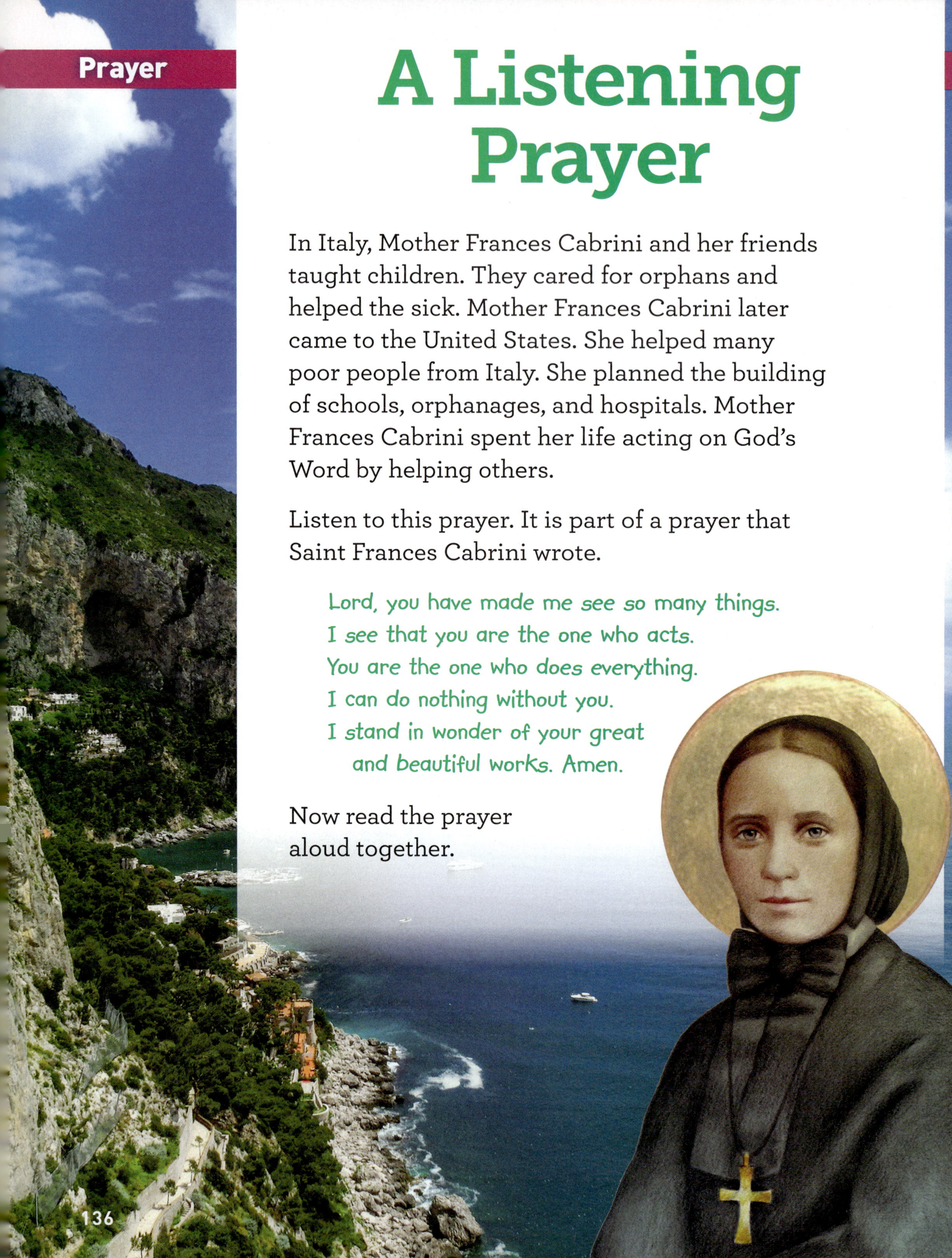

A Listening Prayer

In Italy, Mother Frances Cabrini and her friends taught children. They cared for orphans and helped the sick. Mother Frances Cabrini later came to the United States. She helped many poor people from Italy. She planned the building of schools, orphanages, and hospitals. Mother Frances Cabrini spent her life acting on God's Word by helping others.

Listen to this prayer. It is part of a prayer that Saint Frances Cabrini wrote.

Lord, you have made me see so many things.
I see that you are the one who acts.
You are the one who does everything.
I can do nothing without you.
I stand in wonder of your great
and beautiful works. Amen.

Now read the prayer aloud together.

Chapter Review 11

A **Draw a line** to match each need with an action that responds to God's Word.

1. People are hungry. •	• We give them water.
2. People are thirsty. •	• We give them shelter.
3. People are cold. •	• We take care of them.
4. People are sick. •	• We give them clothes.
5. People are homeless. •	• We give them food.

B **Complete** each sentence with the correct word.

forever	Jesus	Mercy	Word

1. Actions taking care of the needs of others are Works of ____________________.
2. When we help others in loving service, we act as ____________________ did.
3. People who act on God's Word will be with Jesus ____________________.
4. Saint Martin de Porres spent his life acting on God's ____________________.

Faith in Action

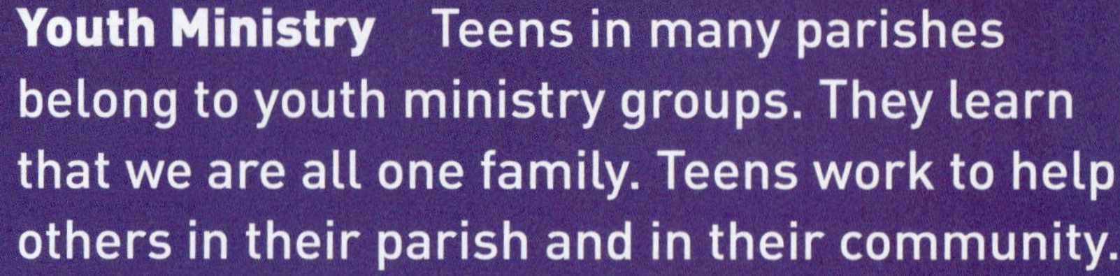

Youth Ministry Teens in many parishes belong to youth ministry groups. They learn that we are all one family. Teens work to help others in their parish and in their community.

In Your Parish

ACTIVITY Think about teens who are part of your parish youth ministry. What are some of the things you see them doing in your parish?

In Everyday Life

ACTIVITY Read the words in each balloon. Circle the word(s) that are about helping. Put the underlined letters from the circled words on the lines.

1
babysit
sleep late

2–3
eat snacks
carry groceries

4–5
visit sick
text with friends

6
litter
recycle

7
act silly
collect food

___ ___ ___ ___ ___ ___ ___
1 2 3 4 5 6 7

Take Home

We Pray for Others

In this chapter, the children will become more aware of the needs of others. They will learn that one way we can help others is by praying for them. When we pray, we trust God to care for people's needs. The children will also compose their own prayers for other people.

ACTIVITY **Trust Walk**

Blindfold one family member. Then have someone be the trust walk leader. It is the leader's job to make sure that the blindfolded person doesn't bump into anything or get hurt. It is the blindfolded person's job to trust the leader. Take turns being the blindfolded person and the leader. Then talk about what it was like to play these roles.

THROUGH THE WEEK

A PRAYER FOR THE WEEK Lord, sometimes we are so concerned with our own needs that we don't pay attention to the needs of those around us. Open our eyes and our hearts to see the needs of others, as did Saint Paula Montal Fornés. Amen.

ON SUNDAY
Listen for the priest to say the words "Let us pray." When he pauses after saying these words, use the moment of silence to be quiet and prayerful.

ON THE WEB
BlestAreWe.com
RCLBLectionary.com
SaintsResource.com

Saint Paula Montal Fornés (1799–1889)

Paula was born in Spain. After her father died, she worked as a seamstress to help her family. With a friend she began a school. She later founded the Daughters of Mary. She was canonized in 2001.

Patron Saint of: seamstresses

Feast Day: February 26

Take Home

Scripture Background
In the Time of Jesus

Prayer The earliest instances of prayer recorded in the Old Testament are conversations God initiates with people. In Genesis, God speaks with Adam (see Genesis 1:28–30) and with Abraham (see Genesis 15:1–21). In Exodus 3:4–22, God speaks with Moses. Christ's role as the mediator between God and humans is shown in the New Testament. Because Jesus is the Second Person of the Holy Trinity, when we pray to him we are praying to God. Prayer is addressed to God the Father through Jesus Christ. This is based on the concept that God's grace and love come through Christ.

You can read of Jesus' role as the mediator in John 1:1–18.

Our Catholic Tradition in Prayer

Novenas "Do not despise my poor prayer. Do not let my trust be confounded!"

This prayer is part of a novena to Saint Jude. Also known as Saint Jude Thaddeus, he is the patron saint of impossible causes.

A novena is a devotion consisting of prayer repeated on nine consecutive days, or once weekly for nine weeks, for a specific intention. The word *novena* comes from the Latin word *novem*, meaning "nine." The devotion reflects the Apostles' experience. They prayed for nine days awaiting the Holy Spirit at Pentecost. Mary is perhaps most often addressed in novenas.

Chapter 12

We Pray for Others

I call upon you; answer me, O God.

Psalm 17:6

Share

Have you ever made a list of things you wish you could do? You might want to learn to ice skate. Maybe you would like to see the ocean.

ACTIVITY

My Wish List

Write three of your wishes here.

1. I wish ______________________________.

2. I wish ______________________________.

3. I wish ______________________________.

What do Church members ask for when they pray?

Hear and Believe **Scripture**

Jesus and Prayer

Jesus taught about the kinds of prayer. He said we should ask God the Father for what we need for ourselves. "Ask, and you shall receive," Jesus said. "Pray for what you need, and God the Father will give it to you."

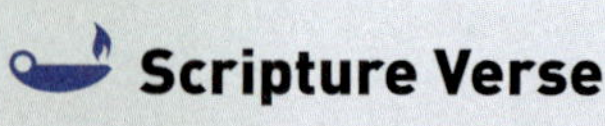

Scripture Verse

"Ask and it will be given to you; . . . "

Matthew 18:20

Jesus also asked us to pray for the needs of other people. "When you come together to pray for others, I will be with you," Jesus promised. "The Father will give you whatever you ask for in my name."

On the night before he died, Jesus ate a special meal with his friends. This meal is called the Last Supper. Jesus blessed bread and wine and it became his Body and Blood. Then he shared it with his friends. Jesus prayed for them. "Father, please keep them safe. Help them to be true to your word."

Based on Matthew 7:7–8; 18:19–20; 26:26–27; John 16:23; 17:9–21

Kinds of Prayer

Jesus told his friends to place their trust in God the Father. When we pray for ourselves, we trust that the Father will answer us. When we pray for other people, we trust that the Father will care for them, too.

Our Church Teaches

At Mass, we pray for our own needs and the needs of others. We ask God the Father to help us be good followers of Jesus. During the Liturgy of the Word we pray the **Prayer of the Faithful**. In this prayer, we pray for people everywhere.

We Believe

We trust our heavenly Father to answer our prayers. We know that God gives us what is truly good for us.

Faith Words

Prayer of the Faithful
During the Prayer of the Faithful we pray for the needs of the Church and of all people. This prayer is the last part of the Liturgy of the Word.

How can we pray for others?

Respond

The Needs of Others

Before we can pray for others, we need to know what they need. The photos on this page tell stories. Talk about what the people need.

How would you ask God to care for these people?

ACTIVITIES

The prayer below is a prayer for people in need.

For those who are sick,
we pray to the Lord.

1. Use your own words to complete these prayers for other people.

   For those who ________________________,
   we pray to the Lord.

   For those who ________________________,
   we pray to the Lord.

2. Color each space that has an X. What is the hidden message?

   ____

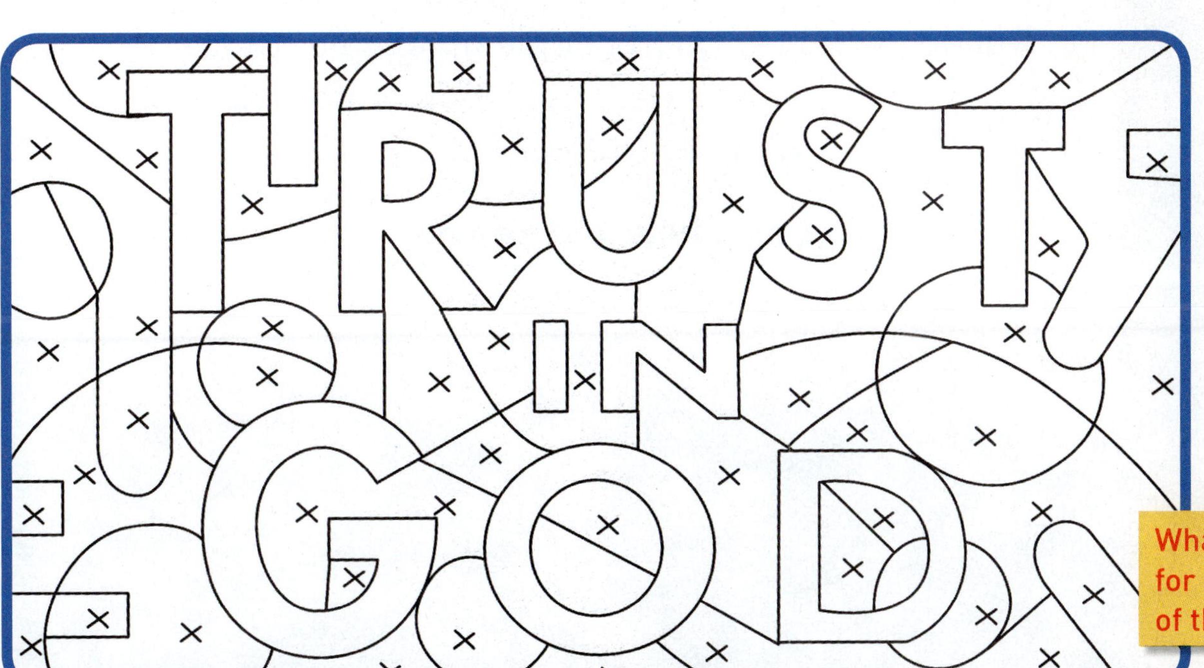

What do we pray for in the Prayer of the Faithful?

Prayer of the Faithful

Leader: As the People of God, we pray for our Church and for the needs of people everywhere.

Reader 1: May all the people in the world know God's love. We pray to the Lord.

All: **Lord, hear our prayer.**

Reader 2: May Church members throughout the world follow Jesus by loving one another. We pray to the Lord.

All: **Lord, hear our prayer.**

Reader 3: May world leaders make good choices to help all people live in peace. We pray to the Lord.

All: **Lord, hear our prayer.**

Reader 4: May good people give aid to those who are hungry, poor, or homeless. We pray to the Lord.

All: **Lord, hear our prayer.**

Chapter Review 12

A **Respond** to the following question.
Who does God the Father want us to follow?

____

____

B **Circle** the best answer to complete each sentence.

1. The ______ is the special meal Jesus ate with his friends on the night before he died.

   Last Supper   lesson   harvest

2. Jesus taught about the kinds of ______.

   Mass   prayer   songs

3. During the ______ we pray for people everywhere.

   Nicene Creed   Prayer of the Faithful   Rosary

4. We ______ God to answer our prayers.

   doubt   trust   wish

5. The Liturgy of the ______ ends with the Prayer of the Faithful.

   Eucharist   Mass   Word

Faith in Action

Prayer Groups Many parishes have prayer groups. People gather together to pray for the needs of those in the parish, the community, and the world. They pray for the sick and homebound members of the parish. They pray for those who have died. They may also pray for the intentions listed in a parish book of intentions.

In Everyday Life

ACTIVITY Think of times when you pray together with other people. Who do you pray with? What do you pray for? Write your own prayer. Share it with your family this week.

____

____

____

____

In Your Parish

ACTIVITY Find these words about prayer groups in your parish.

PRAISE **CHILDREN**
THANKS **ROSARY**
PEACE **HEALING**

N	C	P	J	A	K	M	P
L	Y	R	Q	M	R	V	E
T	H	A	N	K	S	G	A
P	N	I	G	C	R	L	C
R	O	S	A	R	Y	K	E
M	P	E	C	G	Q	V	K
C	H	I	L	D	R	E	N
K	H	E	A	L	I	N	G

We Celebrate the Gift of Eucharist

God the Father's greatest gift to us is his only Son, Jesus Christ. We celebrate the Eucharist to praise and thank God for this gift. We celebrate to share more fully in the life of Christ.

> . . . "I am the bread of life; whoever comes to me will never hunger, and whoever believes in me will never thirst."
>
> John 6:35

Jesus was buried in a tomb very much like the one shown here. We remember Jesus' Death and Resurrection each time we receive Holy Communion.

SONG

Eat This Bread

John 6, Adapted by Robert J. Batastini and the Taizé Community

Music by Jacques Berthier

© 1984, Les Presses de Taizé, GIA Publications, Inc., agent.

Getting ready for Chapter 13

Take Home

Jesus Saves Us from Sin

This chapter presents the story of Jesus' Death and Resurrection. The children will consider the concept of sacrifice as it applies to everyday life, and they will learn about the ultimate sacrifice Jesus made when he gave up his life so that we could have eternal life.

ACTIVITY **The Rugged Cross**

Work together to make a cross of twigs held together with a piece of twine or a pipe cleaner. Display your work in a prominent place. Let it serve as a reminder that Jesus sacrificed his life to save us from sin.

THROUGH THE WEEK

A PRAYER FOR THE WEEK Jesus, help us to be like Saint Elizabeth and make sacrifices to care for others. May our efforts be a way to thank you for sacrificing your life to save us. Amen.

ON SUNDAY

After the words of consecration, sing the Memorial Acclamation with a renewed sense of appreciation for all that Christ has done for you.

ON THE WEB

BlestAreWe.com

RCLBLectionary.com

SaintsResource.com

Saint Elizabeth of Hungary (1207–1231)

Elizabeth was born a princess in Hungary. She lived a simple life and devoted herself to her family and to works of charity. Money and fame were not important to her.

Patron Saint of:
homeless people and exiles

Feast Day:
November 17

Take Home

Scripture Background

In the Time of Jesus

Crucifixion The most wretched of deaths, crucifixion, was reserved for criminals involved in serious crimes. It was an act of treason for Jesus to be considered a king, an act meriting crucifixion in the eyes of first-century Romans. The letters of Paul, however, identify the Cross as a symbol of victory. By it, we have been set free and redeemed from the power of sin.

You can read of Jesus' Crucifixion in Mark 15:22–26, and Paul's interpretation of it in 1 Corinthians 1:19–25.

Our Catholic Tradition in World Ministries

Congregation of Holy Cross Father Basil Anthony Moreau was born in 1799, near the end of the French Revolution. At age 22 he was ordained a priest. There was an urgent need to minister to Catholics in France. Father Moreau gathered a group of priests and brothers to establish the Congregation of Holy Cross in 1837. Today four congregations follow his spirit and ministry: the Congregation of Holy Cross, the Marianites of Holy Cross, the Sisters of the Holy Cross, and Sisters of Holy Cross. They minister worldwide.

In 2007, Pope John Paul II beatified Father Basil Moreau. Beatification is the final step toward sainthood.

Jesus Saves Us from Sin

Chapter 13

"No one has greater love than this, to lay down one's life for one's friends." John 15:13

Share

Acting on God's Word is not always easy.
Sometimes we have to give up what we want.
Sometimes we have to put the needs of others first.

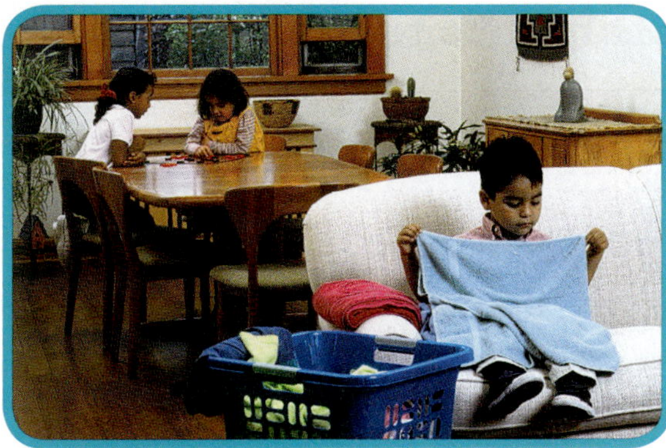

What is the boy giving up?
Why is he doing this?

What is the girl giving up?
Why is she doing this?

ACTIVITY

Draw a picture of a time you gave up something to help another person.

What did Jesus give up for us?

Hear and Believe **Scripture**

 Jesus Gives Up His Life

Jesus was arrested the night he shared a special meal with his friends. This was on the feast of Passover. Jesus changed the bread and wine to be his Body and Blood. This changed the meaning of Passover for Christians forever.

The next morning, soldiers gave Jesus a wooden cross to carry. Then they put Jesus to death on the Cross.

After Jesus died, some of his friends took his body away. They placed his body in a tomb.

Three days later, some women friends went to the tomb. When they got there, the tomb was empty. An angel told the friends that Jesus had been raised from the dead.

Based on Mark 14:22–52; 15:22–47; 16:1–6

Scripture Verse

. . . "Truly this man was the Son of God!"

Mark 15:39

God's Gift of Jesus

Jesus is God the Father's greatest gift to us. Jesus gave up his life as a **sacrifice** for our sins. A sacrifice is a special gift that is given out of love.

We call Jesus our Savior. A **savior** is someone who rescues others. Jesus died on the Cross to rescue, or to save, us from our sins.

Our Church Teaches

Three days after Jesus' Death, God raised Jesus to new life. By his life, Death, and **Resurrection**, Jesus showed us God's love. We received the promise of new life. On Easter we celebrate Jesus' Resurrection.

We Believe

Because of Jesus' Death and Resurrection, we too can have eternal life.

Faith Words

sacrifice
A sacrifice is a special gift that is given out of love.

savior
A savior is someone who rescues others.

Resurrection
The Resurrection is Jesus' being raised from the dead to new life.

In what ways can we show love through sacrifice?

Respond

Saint Elizabeth of Hungary

Elizabeth was born a long, long time ago. She was the daughter of the king and queen of Hungary. Elizabeth was rich, and she spent her money wisely.

Elizabeth loved Jesus very much. To show her love, she fed people who were poor and hungry. She took care of people who were sick and alone. Because of Elizabeth, hospitals were built in two towns. Elizabeth sold her fancy clothes and jewelry to help the poor. She gave everything she had to people in need.

Why did Saint Elizabeth of Hungary make sacrifices?

ACTIVITIES

1. Think of one sacrifice you could make this week. Write about how this sacrifice will show your love for someone.

2. Write or draw about a time someone made a sacrifice to show their love for you.

In what way can we celebrate the sacrifice of Jesus?

A Prayer of Faith

Leader: During the Mass we remember Jesus' sacrifice for us. The priest says, "The mystery of faith." We respond with a special prayer of faith.

All: **We proclaim your Death, O Lord, and profess your Resurrection until you come again.**

Roman Missal

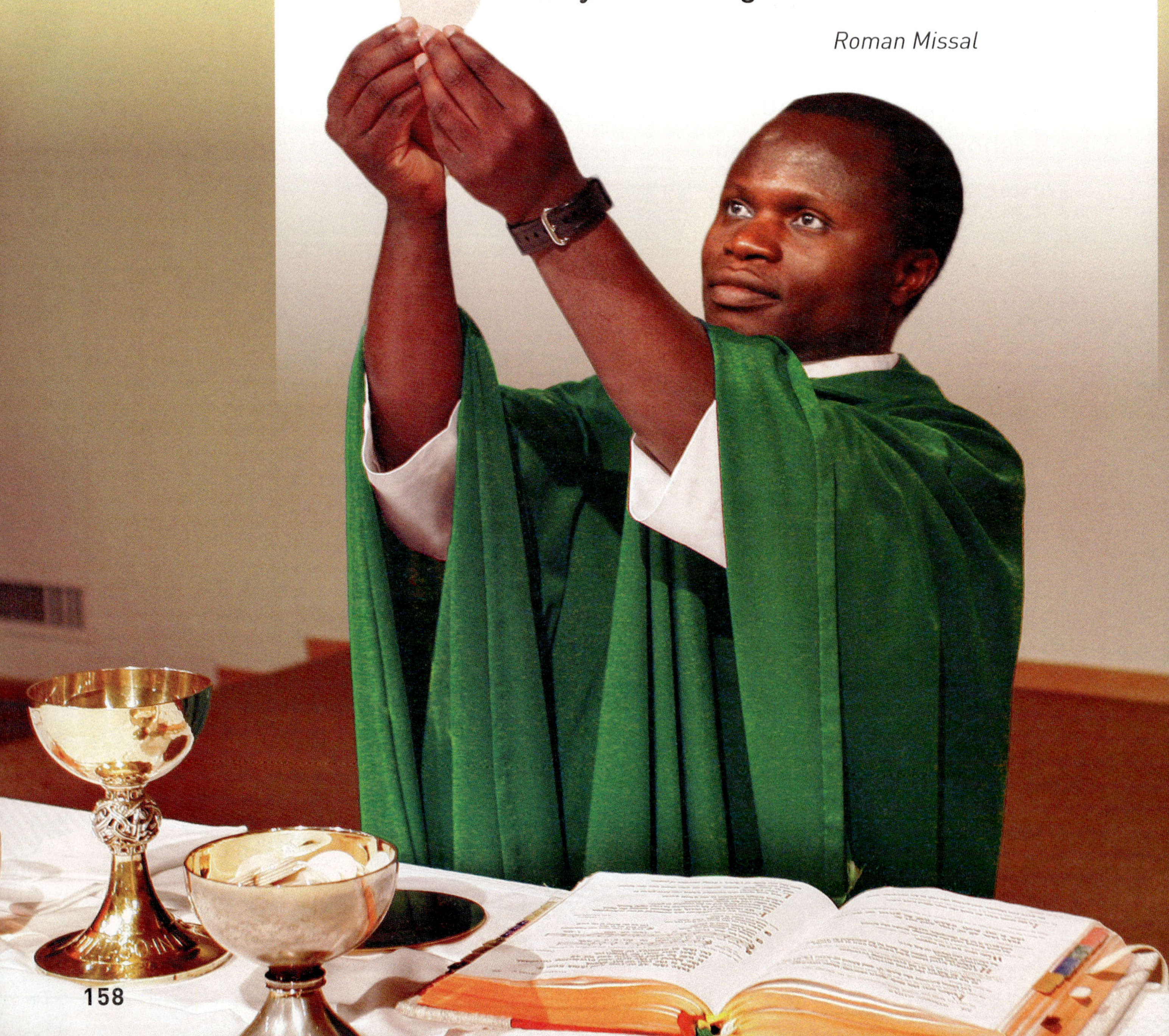

Chapter Review 13

A **Draw a line** to connect the parts of each sentence.

1. Giving up something we want out of love is ______. •	• someone who rescues others.
2. Jesus is ______. •	• called a sacrifice.
3. A savior is ______. •	• God's greatest gift to us.

B **Complete** the sentences with words from the box.

come	Death	Jesus	Resurrection

1. During Mass, we remember that ______________ died and was raised from the dead.
2. Complete this prayer from the Mass.

"We proclaim your ______________, O Lord,

and profess your ______________

until you ______________ again."

Faith in Action

Welcome Ministry The Catholic Church has members from all over the world. Parish members are called to make all feel welcome, even those who may have just come to this country. The welcome ministry at your parish may organize fairs, picnics, or special gatherings as a way to reach out and help new families.

In Your Parish

ACTIVITY Think about people who have joined your parish community. How has your parish made them feel welcome? On a separate piece of paper, draw one example of making them feel welcome.

In Everyday Life

ACTIVITY Unscramble the words below. Use them to finish the sentence. Think of ways you can do what it says at home and at school this week.

LAL KETA

We ___ ___ ___ are called to ___ ___ ___ ___

ERCA OHTRE

___ ___ ___ ___ of each ___ ___ ___ ___ ___.

Getting ready for Chapter 14

Take Home

We Receive the Gift of Jesus

This chapter presents the concept of the Real Presence of Jesus in the Eucharist. The children will learn that we remember the Last Supper at Mass. They will discover that Jesus is present in the Eucharist. Lastly, they will learn how to receive Jesus in the Eucharist.

ACTIVITY **It's All Set**

Teach your child how to set the table with plates, glasses, napkins, and silverware. Add candles and flowers. Explain that just as the family table should be set in a particular way for a meal, so the altar is set in a particular way for Mass.

THROUGH THE WEEK

A PRAYER FOR THE WEEK O Lord, we give thanks for the great gift of the Eucharist. Just as Jesus shared this greatest of gifts with us, may we in turn share our gifts with others. Amen.

ON SUNDAY
Listen carefully to the words of consecration. After Mass, discuss what you heard.

ON THE WEB
BlestAreWe.com
RCLBLectionary.com
SaintsResource.com

Saint Teresa of the Andes (1900–1920)

Born Juanita Solar in Santiago, Chile, Saint Teresa joined the Carmelites at age 19. From childhood, she focused her life on sacrifice and prayer. At the age of 20 she died from typhoid fever. In 1993, she became the first Chilean to be canonized.

Patron Saint of:
sick people and all young people

Feast Day: July 13

Take Home

Scripture Background
In the Time of Jesus

Passover Meal When Jesus and the Apostles gathered for a meal on the night before he died, they were sharing a Passover meal to commemorate the freedom of the Jews from Egyptian slavery. Foods at a Passover meal have special meaning. The matzo, or unleavened bread, represents manna, which fed the Israelites in the desert; bitter herbs symbolize the harshness of slavery; the lamb recalls the sacrifice at the first Passover; and the egg symbolizes new life in the covenant with God.

You can read about Jesus' Last Supper in Matthew 26:17–30.

Our Catholic Tradition in Rituals

Eucharistic Processions Many parishes and dioceses celebrate a Eucharistic procession on the Solemnity of the Most Holy Body and Blood of Christ. The Blessed Sacrament is displayed in a monstrance and is carried in a procession around the church, from one parish to another, or—with the permission of the diocesan bishop—through the neighborhood of the church. Often, a canopy is held over the priest or bishop holding the monstrance. Eucharistic hymns are sung during the procession, which often stops at four stations for the proclamation of a Gospel reading, a prayer, and a blessing. At the conclusion of the procession, benediction is celebrated. Such processions give public witness to Catholics' devotion to the Eucharist and belief in the Real Presence of Christ in the Eucharist.

We Receive the Gift of Jesus

Chapter 14

. . . "I am the bread of life; whoever comes to me will never hunger, . . ." John 6:35

Share

We all need food and water to stay healthy. But we have other needs, or hungers, too.

ACTIVITY

Look at these pictures. How is each person hungry?

Matt has not eaten since lunch. He is hungry for ______________________.

Chloe is very, very tired. She is hungry for ______________________.

Luis can't rake all these leaves. He is hungry for ______________________.

In what ways does Jesus answer our needs and hungers?

Hear and Believe Worship

The Gift of Eucharist

The second part of the Mass is the Liturgy of the Eucharist. We offer gifts of bread and wine. We remember the Last Supper. The priest prepares the gifts that will become the Body and Blood of Christ. He then prays:

On the day before he was to suffer,
on the night of the Last Supper,
he took bread and said the blessing,
broke the bread and gave it to his disciples, saying:

TAKE THIS, ALL OF YOU, AND EAT OF IT,
FOR THIS IS MY BODY,
WHICH WILL BE GIVEN UP FOR YOU.

In a similar way, when supper was ended,
he took the chalice, gave you thanks
and gave the chalice to his disciples, saying:

TAKE THIS, ALL OF YOU, AND DRINK FROM IT,
FOR THIS IS THE CHALICE OF MY BLOOD,
THE BLOOD OF THE NEW AND ETERNAL COVENANT,
WHICH WILL BE POURED OUT FOR YOU AND FOR MANY
FOR THE FORGIVENESS OF SINS.
DO THIS IN MEMORY OF ME.

Eucharistic Prayer for Use in Masses for Various Needs II
Roman Missal

The Meal of God's People

During Mass we remember the Last Supper. At that meal, Jesus changed bread and wine into his Body and Blood. At Mass we also remember the Death and Resurrection of Jesus Christ.

The Mass is a holy meal for the People of God today. At Mass Jesus gives us himself in the **Eucharist**. Through the Holy Spirit, bread and wine become the Body and Blood of Jesus Christ. We give thanks for Jesus' sacrifice.

GO TO pages 269-270 to learn more about the Liturgy of the Eucharist.

Our Church Teaches

Only a priest can preside over, or lead, the celebration of the Eucharist. We receive the Body and Blood of Christ in **Holy Communion**. The Eucharist unites us with Jesus, the Bread of Life. He strengthens us.

We Believe

In Holy Communion, Christ gives us himself, the Bread of Life.

Faith Words

Eucharist
The Eucharist is a sacrifice and a special meal of thanks.

Holy Communion
We receive the Body and Blood of Christ in Holy Communion

Scripture Verse

. . . [H]e took bread, said the blessing, broke it, and gave it to them.

Luke 24:30

What do Catholics do when they receive Holy Communion?

Respond

Going to Communion

Sister Christine was meeting with a group of girls and boys. She said, "Tell me what you know about receiving Holy Communion."

Every hand in the group shot up!

Paolo answered first. "I must have already received Penance and Reconciliation before my First Communion. I must be free of serious sin," he said.

Lucy said, "I shouldn't eat or drink anything but water for one hour before receiving Communion."

"I can receive Communion either in my hand or on my tongue," added April.

"The priest, deacon, or extraordinary minister of Holy Communion says, 'The Body of Christ.' Then I bow and answer 'Amen,'" said Mike.

"Then I am offered the Blood of Christ from the cup," said Trish, "and I bow and answer 'Amen' again."

José said, "After Communion, I return to my place in church. I give thanks because I have received the gift of the Eucharist."

"Wow!" said Sister. "You didn't forget a thing!"

If you have celebrated First Eucharist, what do you do after receiving Holy Communion?

ACTIVITY

Cross out each **Q, X,** or **Z** in the puzzle.

Complete the sentence with words you found in the puzzle. Jesus told his followers,

____

____

In what ways can we celebrate being one with Jesus?

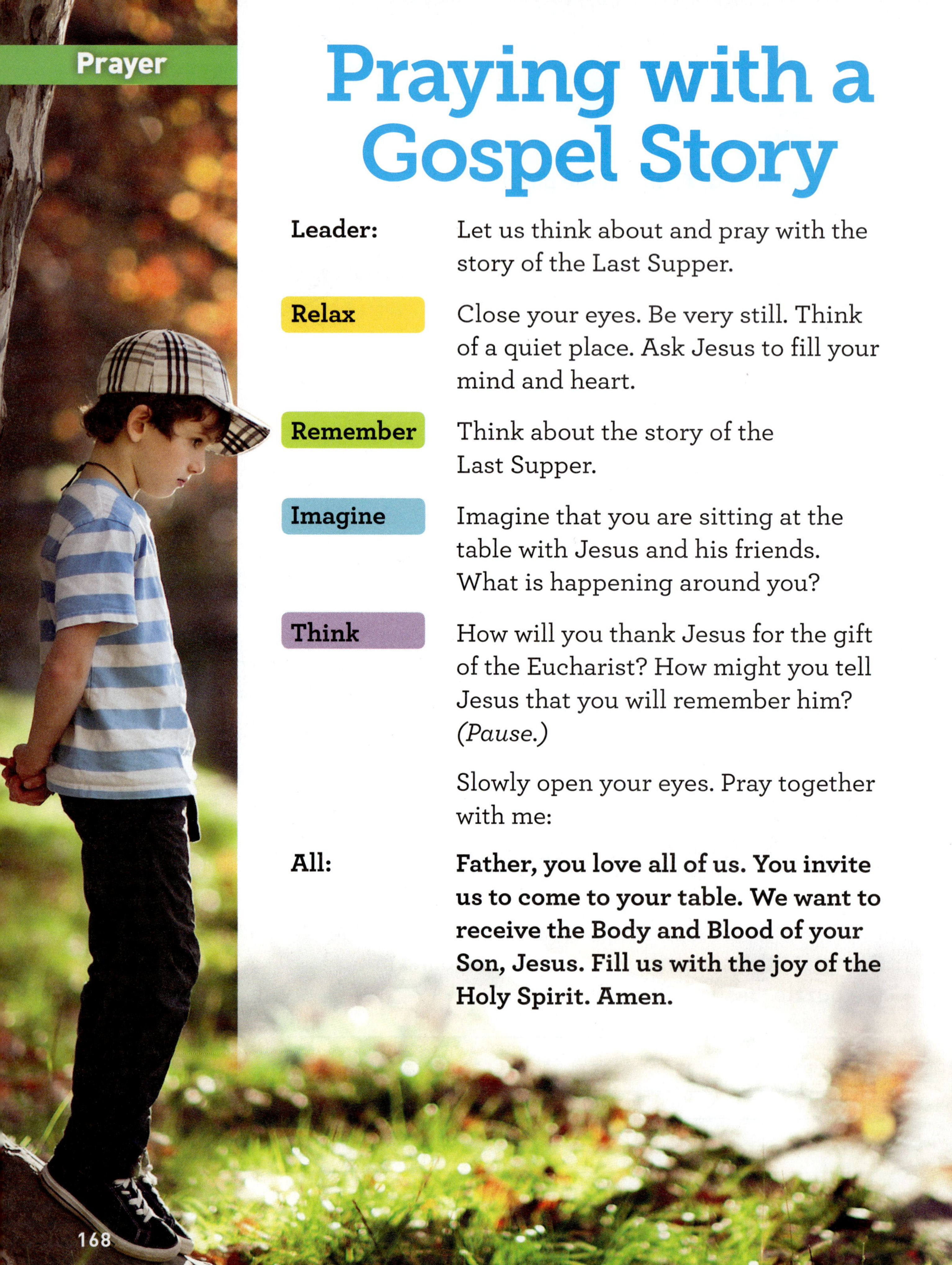

Prayer

Praying with a Gospel Story

Leader: Let us think about and pray with the story of the Last Supper.

Relax Close your eyes. Be very still. Think of a quiet place. Ask Jesus to fill your mind and heart.

Remember Think about the story of the Last Supper.

Imagine Imagine that you are sitting at the table with Jesus and his friends. What is happening around you?

Think How will you thank Jesus for the gift of the Eucharist? How might you tell Jesus that you will remember him? *(Pause.)*

Slowly open your eyes. Pray together with me:

All: **Father, you love all of us. You invite us to come to your table. We want to receive the Body and Blood of your Son, Jesus. Fill us with the joy of the Holy Spirit. Amen.**

Chapter Review 14

A **Complete** the definition

During the ______________________________
we remember and give thanks for Jesus' sacrifice of himself.

B **Draw a line** to match the descriptions with the correct words.

1. Another name for receiving the Body and Blood of Christ	• in the hand
2. Our answer when the minister of Communion says "The Body of Christ" or "The Blood of Christ"	• the Last Supper
3. One way to receive the Body of Christ	• Amen
4. Who presides, or leads, the Eucharist	• Holy Communion
5. What we remember during the Liturgy of the Eucharist	• the priest

Faith in Action

Extraordinary Ministers of Holy Communion Extraordinary ministers of Holy Communion distribute Communion at Mass or take the Eucharist to people who are sick or homebound. They pray with them and comfort them. These ministers show respect for each person they serve.

In Everyday Life

ACTIVITY Write one way you will show respect for someone you will serve this week.

____

____

In Your Parish

ACTIVITY Write the letter for the missing word in each sentence.

A. Eucharist B. gift C. priests D. respect E. serve

1. All who give out Holy Communion show _____ for others.
2. Deacons and _____ also give out Holy Communion.
3. Ministers of Holy Communion take the _____ to others.
4. All ministers of Holy Communion _____ people.
5. In the Eucharist, we receive the _____ of Christ.

Getting ready for Chapter 15

Take Home

We Carry On the Work of Jesus

Chapter 15 presents the New Commandment that Jesus gave us about loving one another. The children will discover how Jesus showed his love for people. They will also identify ways that they can show their love for others.

ACTIVITY **Choose One Task**

With your child's help, think of different tasks any family member could do, such as putting away toys or folding towels. Together, write the tasks on slips of paper, fold them, and place them in a bowl. Then have each person take one slip from the bowl each day and complete the task.

THROUGH THE WEEK

A PRAYER FOR THE WEEK Through her works, Lord, Saint Marianne shared your love with others. Help us carry on good works with acts of kindness, healing, and love. Amen.

ON SUNDAY
As you pray silently before the Prayer after Communion, reflect on how you will love others as Jesus loves you.

ON THE WEB
BlestAreWe.com
RCLBLectionary.com
SaintsResource.com

Saint Marianne Cope of Molokai (1838–1918)

Marianne was born in Germany. She joined Father Damien on the island of Molokai and remained there for thirty-five years working with young leprosy patients. She was canonized in 2012.

Patron Saint of: victims of leprosy, those with HIV/AIDS

Feast Day January 23

Take Home

Scripture Background
In the Time of Jesus

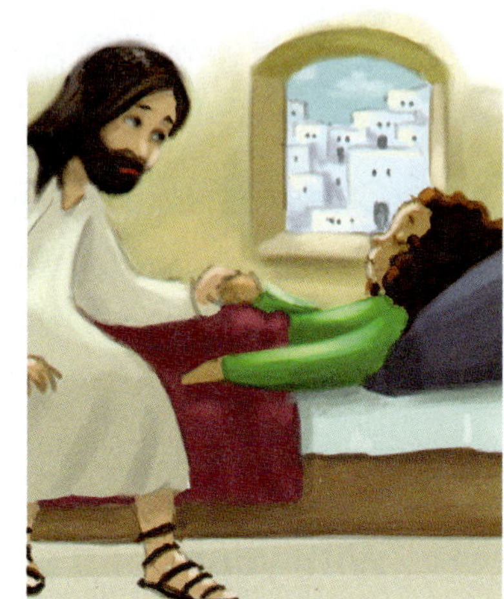

Illness and Sin Even in the time of ancient Israel, people sensed that there was some sort of link between the sin and evil of the world and the illness and suffering they saw around them. Some incorrectly judged that their sin and suffering were a result of God's vengeance, just as some do today. But God, who is all-good, can never cause evil. All the sin, suffering, and hardship in the world exists as the effect of Original Sin and the continued sinfulness of ourselves and others. When Jesus healed those who were sick in body or in spirit, he did so to show them God's love, and to reveal that in Jesus himself sin and evil were being overcome. Today we are called to continue the work of Jesus by helping the power of good to overcome suffering in the world.

You can read of Jesus' healing acts in Mark 5:21–42.

Our Catholic Tradition in Religious Life

Saint Damien de Veuster Damien de Veuster, also known as Damien of Molokai, was a holy person who risked his life caring for others. Born Joseph de Veuster in Belgium in 1840, he joined the Sacred Heart Fathers as a young man, taking the name Damien. After ordination to the priesthood, he served in the Hawaiian missions. In 1866, a sickness known as leprosy spread across the Hawaiian Islands. Lepers were exiled to the island of Molokai. Father Damien volunteered to minister to them. He took care of them and built houses, hospitals, and churches for them. He contracted leprosy in 1885 and died in 1889. Pope Benedict XVI named Father Damien a saint of the Church in 2009.

We Carry On the Work of Jesus

Chapter 15

Love one another as I have loved you.

Based on John 13:34

Share

What kinds of workers do you see?

What kind of work would you like to do when you grow up? Show it in a drawing.

What work did Jesus do?

Hear and Believe **Scripture**

Jesus and the Little Girl

Storyteller:	One day Jesus was speaking to a crowd of people. A man named Jairus was there.
Jairus:	*(kneels in front of Jesus)* Lord, please come to my home. Please help my sick daughter.
Jesus:	Show me the way. I will help her.
Jairus:	*(gets up)* Thank you, Jesus. Let's go!
Storyteller:	They started walking. A servant from the house of Jairus ran up to them.
Servant:	Sir, your daughter just died.
Storyteller:	Jairus was very sad.
Jesus:	Do not worry, Jairus. Just have faith.
Storyteller:	When they got to the house, Jesus went in. The dead girl was lying on the bed.
Jesus:	*(taking her hand)* Little girl, get up!
Storyteller:	The little girl got up at once. They were amazed!

Based on Mark 5:21–24, 35–42

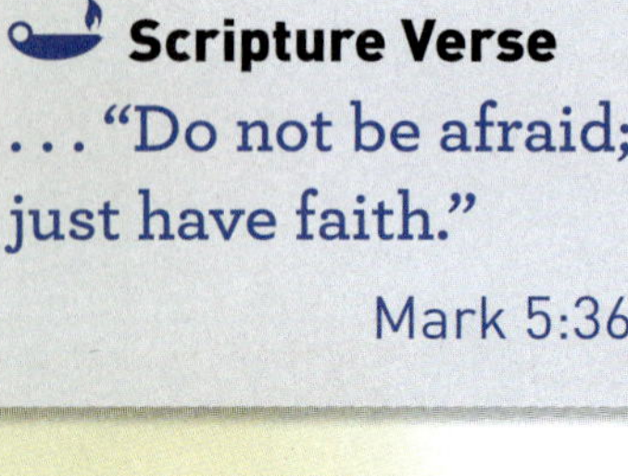

Scripture Verse

. . . "Do not be afraid; just have faith."

Mark 5:36

The Work of Jesus

In this Bible story, Jesus showed his love for Jairus and his daughter. Jesus taught people about God's love for everyone. He did this in many ways. He told stories. He shared food. He forgave sinners. He comforted sad people. Jesus healed the sick. He even brought dead people back to life.

Our Church Teaches

In the **New Commandment** Jesus said, "Love one another as I have loved you." This is the law of love. We are called to love others the way God loves us. When we show our love for others we also show our love for God.

We Believe

When we love others, we are following Jesus. We are also showing our love for God.

Faith Words

New Commandment
The New Commandment from Jesus is, "Love one another as I have loved you."

What are some everyday ways we can love others?

Respond Taking Care of Others

"Mrs. Nye wasn't at Mass Sunday," said Mattie. "She is home, sick and alone. She can't even cook!

"Everybody wanted to help. Dr. Ray stopped in to see Mrs. Nye. Joey Garcia brought her a nice lunch. He stayed and visited for a while. The Grant family prepared her dinner."

"So that took care of Sunday. What about the rest of the week?" asked Kim.

Mattie answered, "Parish members will take meals to Mrs. Nye every day."

"Let's ask everybody in the parish to pray for her, too," added Kim.

"You know, Jesus taught us to love one another as he loved us. When we care for Mrs. Nye, we show our love for God!"

ACTIVITIES

Show how you can carry on the work of Jesus.

1. Write something you might say to someone who is sad.

____

____

2. Draw a picture that shows how you can help a sick person.

In what way can we pray a simple prayer for others?

A Thumb Prayer for Others

You can pray for others by using a thumb prayer. Trace a small sign of a cross with your thumb. On the downward stroke of the cross, think "Jesus." On the sideways stroke, think the name of someone you are praying for.

You might pray ⇩ "Jesus," then ⇨ "Uncle Jim." Trace your thumb cross in the palm of your hand, on a book, or anywhere.

Choose one of the thumb prayers below. Say your prayer over and over.

⇩ Jesus ⇨ the pope

⇩ Jesus ⇨ all parents

⇩ Jesus ⇨ those in need

⇩ Jesus ⇨ our pastor

⇩ Jesus ⇨ all children

⇩ Jesus ⇨ (your own prayer)

"Thumb Prayer" adapted from *Catechist* magazine. © Page McKean Zyromski, contributing editor.

Chapter Review 15

A **Circle** the best answer.

1. How can we follow Jesus?

   We can fight. We can sin. We can show love.

2. "Love one another as I have loved you."
   What do we call this law?

   Ten Commandments Creed New Commandment

3. Who did Jesus forgive?

   all people sad people sinful people

4. In the Thumb Prayer, what sign do you make?

   sign of a cross sign of peace stop sign

B **Draw or write** about ways to love others as Jesus did.

Faith in Action

Parish Nurse Many parishes have a parish nurse. This person serves the whole parish community. The nurse helps people find health services. This nurse visits the sick to help them heal. Some parish nurses teach classes on health care.

In Your Parish

ACTIVITY Use the code to write the missing letters.

A	B	C	D	E	F	G	H	I	L	N	O	R	S	T
1	2	3	4	5	6	7	8	9	10	11	12	13	14	15

A parish nurse helps people with

H __ __ __ __ H
8 5 1 10 15 8

and H __ __ __ __ __ G.
8 5 1 10 9 11 7

In Everyday Life

ACTIVITY Think about a nurse in your parish and how he or she has helped those who are sick. Draw a picture that shows how you or someone you know can care for someone who is ill.

Getting ready for Chapter 16

Take Home

We Pray Like Jesus

We call God our Father because Jesus taught us to. We pray the Lord's Prayer because Jesus taught it to us. In Chapter 16, the children learn to pray the Lord's Prayer with an understanding of its meaning. The children will also identify the parts of the day during which they might pray.

ACTIVITY **Daily Bread**

The bread that we eat every day may be very different from the bread Jesus ate, or from the breads eaten in other parts of the world. Serve a variety of breads this week (raisin, pita, sourdough, French, Italian, cornbread). Talk about how daily bread is needed by everyone.

THROUGH THE WEEK

A PRAYER FOR THE WEEK Lord, just as Saint Francis Solano prayed with music and song, help us learn many ways to pray to you. No matter how we pray, help us to pray always with an open heart. Amen.

ON SUNDAY

At Mass, say a prayer of gratitude for the Bread of Life, the Eucharist.

ON THE WEB

BlestAreWe.com

RCLBLectionary.com

SaintsResource.com

Saint Francis Solano (1549–1610)

Francis Solano was born in Spain. He became a missionary to the New World in 1589. Father Francis traveled throughout South America, but especially around Lima, Peru, ministering to Indians and Spanish colonists. He often played the violin and sang before the altar.

Patron Saint of: Chile and Peru

Feast Day: July 14

Take Home

Scripture Background

Before the Time of Jesus

Synagogues In Old Testament times there was only one Temple, and it was in Jerusalem. There, Jews prayed and made sacrificial offerings. Synagogues, however, were spread throughout the Holy Land. Here, Jews assembled to pray, read Scripture, and hear teachings based on that Scripture. Prayers often focused on readings from the Pentateuch (the first five books of the Bible) and the prophets. Two central prayers in Judaism—the *Shema* and the *Amidah*—were also prayed.

You can read Isaiah 61:1–2 to reflect on the Scripture Jesus later prayed in a synagogue.

Medieval illumination of Jesus' entry into Jerusalem

Our Catholic Tradition in Symbols

Blessed Palms In Jesus' time, people sometimes used objects as they prayed. Palm branches were used during prayers of praise. The waving branches symbolized victory. Jesus' followers held palm branches during his triumphant entry into Jerusalem before his Passion and Death.

Palms are blessed at the beginning of the Palm Sunday liturgy. The ashes crossed on our forehead on Ash Wednesday come from burned palms. Some families place palms around a hanging crucifix or holy picture. Another tradition is braiding palms into crosses.

We Pray Like Jesus

Chapter 16

I will bless the LORD at all times;
his praise shall be always in my mouth. Psalm 34:2

Share

Many people do things at the same time each day.

At 7:00 a.m., Olivia wakes up.
What time do you usually wake up?

At 8:00 a.m., Michael gets on the bus.
What time do you go to school?

At 6:00 p.m., the Diaz family eats dinner.
What time does your family eat dinner?

Talk about what time things happen on Saturday.
Tell what is different about Sunday.

How did Jesus pray?

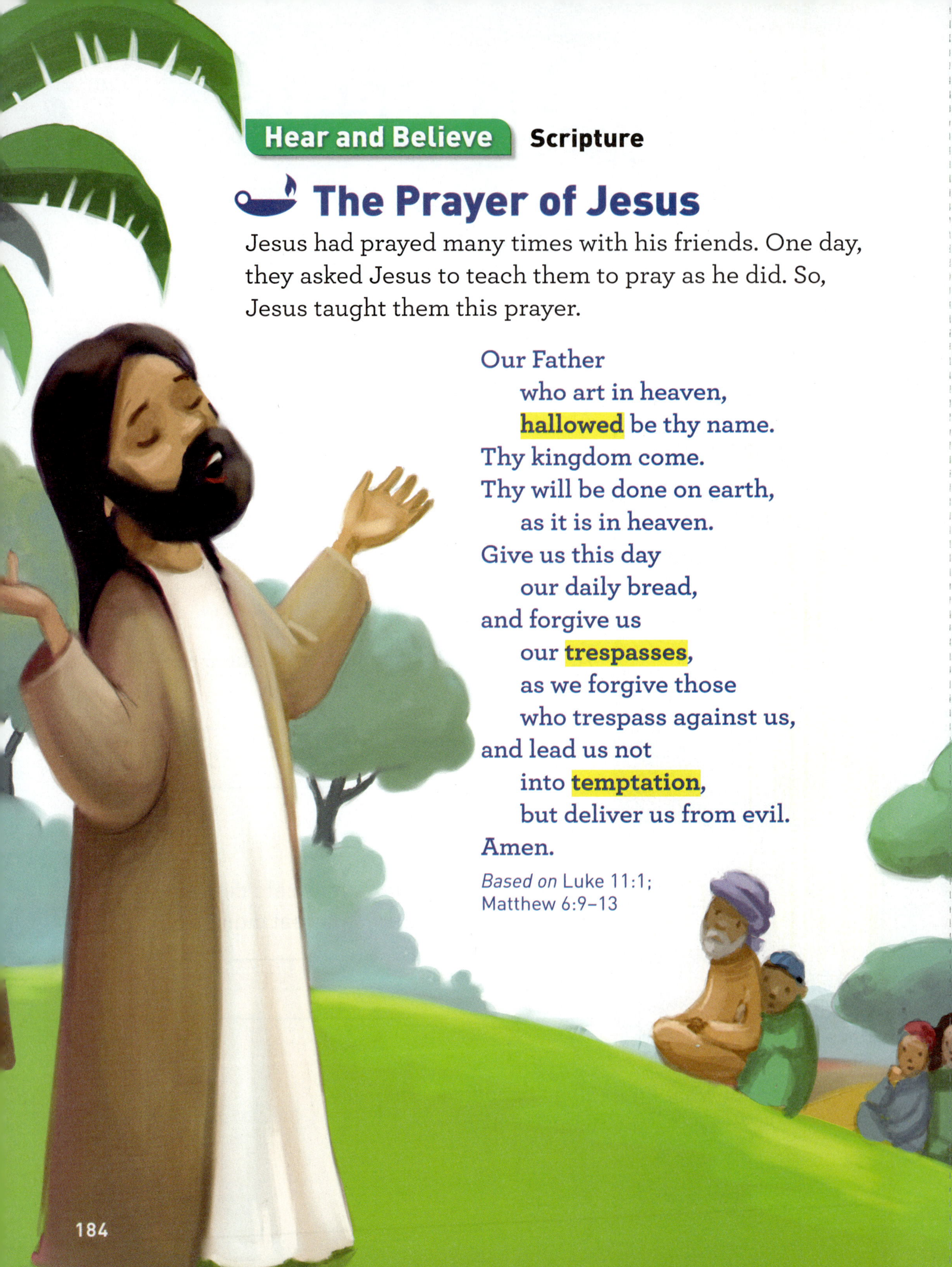

Hear and Believe **Scripture**

The Prayer of Jesus

Jesus had prayed many times with his friends. One day, they asked Jesus to teach them to pray as he did. So, Jesus taught them this prayer.

Our Father
who art in heaven,
hallowed be thy name.
Thy kingdom come.
Thy will be done on earth,
as it is in heaven.
Give us this day
our daily bread,
and forgive us
our **trespasses**,
as we forgive those
who trespass against us,
and lead us not
into **temptation**,
but deliver us from evil.
Amen.

Based on Luke 11:1; Matthew 6:9–13

The Lord's Prayer

We call the prayer Jesus taught the **Lord's Prayer**. Jesus said that God's name is *hallowed,* or "holy." We show respect for God's name. In the Lord's Prayer we remember that God is the Father of all people.

Our Church Teaches

The Lord's Prayer is special because Jesus taught it to us. In it we call God "Father." We ask forgiveness for our sins, our trespasses. We ask that we not have temptations. We do not want to do wrong. At every Mass we pray the Lord's Prayer. When we pray this prayer at Mass, we may hold out our open hands.

We Believe

Jesus taught us to pray the Lord's Prayer. It is the prayer of Christians all over the world.

Faith Words

hallowed
Hallowed is another word for holy.

trespasses
Trespasses are sins or wrongs.

temptation
A temptation is wanting to do something that is wrong.

In what ways do Church members pray?

Respond

Praying Together

Mary and Joseph taught Jesus how to pray. They prayed at home and in the Temple. Our parents teach us how to pray. We pray together at home and in church. As Church members we pray the Lord's Prayer together.

The Lord's Prayer	What It Means
Our Father, who art in heaven, hallowed be thy name;	We praise God the Father for being good and holy.
thy kingdom come, thy will be done on earth as it is in heaven.	We pray God will bring about a time of perfect happiness and peace. We pray that everyone will obey God.
Give us this day our daily bread,	We pray for our needs and the needs of others.
and forgive us our trespasses, as we forgive those who trespass against us;	We ask God to forgive our sins. We forgive people who have hurt us.
and lead us not into temptation,	We ask God to help us choose right instead of wrong.
but deliver us from evil.	We ask God to protect us from things that may harm us.
Amen.	We say, "Yes, I believe. It is true."

ACTIVITIES

1. We can pray the Lord's Prayer at any time during the day. Look at each picture. Decide what time of day it might be. Then place the time on the clocks.

2. Draw yourself praying the Lord's Prayer at another time of day.

What do we ask for in the Lord's Prayer?

A Community Prayer

Leader: Jesus taught us the Lord's Prayer. This prayer to God the Father is a gift from Jesus to us.

All: *(Hold hands out, palms up.)*

Reader 1: We pray "Our Father."
May all your people praise you.

All: *(Take right hand up to mouth.)*

Reader 2: We ask for daily bread.
Please give us what we need this day.

All: *(Bow head, hands down.)*

Reader 3: We ask to be forgiven of our trespasses. Help us remember our promise to forgive others.

All: *(Cross hands in front of face, palms out.)*

Reader 4: We ask to be delivered from evil.
Protect us from harm.

All: **Amen.**

(Share a handshake of peace.)

Chapter Review 16

A **Complete** the sentences with words from the box.

bread	holy	Mass

1. Hallowed means ______________________.

2. We pray the Lord's Prayer at every ______________________.

3. We pray for our daily ______________________.

B **Complete** the correct answer.

1. Jesus taught the ________ to his followers.

   Hail Mary **Sign of the Cross** **Lord's Prayer**

2. Sins or wrongs we do on purpose are ________.

   trespasses **deeds** **grace**

3. Wanting to do something wrong is called ________.

   blessed **temptation** **hallowed**

4. We ask God to deliver us from ________.

   evil **goodness** **prayer**

5. Jesus taught us to call God our ________.

   Son **Brother** **Father**

6. A word that means "holy" is ________

   prayer **hallowed** **Mass**

Faith in Action

Catechists The Holy Spirit calls men and women to be catechists. These are prayerful people who live their faith. Catechists teach religious education. Catechists try to help others grow in their faith. Families work with catechists to prepare their children for the Sacraments.

In Your Parish

ACTIVITY Color the shapes with a cross blue. Color all other shapes yellow. Catechists help us to grow in our __________.

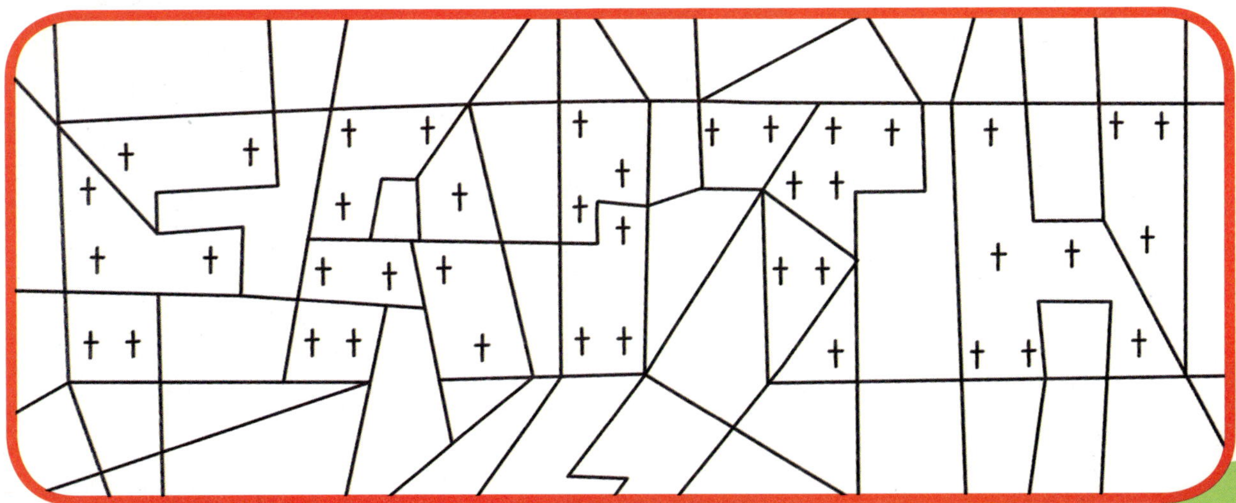

In Everyday Life

ACTIVITY Think of other people who teach you. Name these people and tell what you learn from them.

Unit 5

We Go in Peace

Made stronger by the Eucharist, we work to be more like Christ in all we do. We can help others know about Jesus by the way we treat them.

Blessed are the peacemakers,
for they will be called children of God.

Matthew 5:9

Christ's first disciples may have walked this street in Jerusalem spreading a message of peace. At the end of Mass we also go in peace to serve all people.

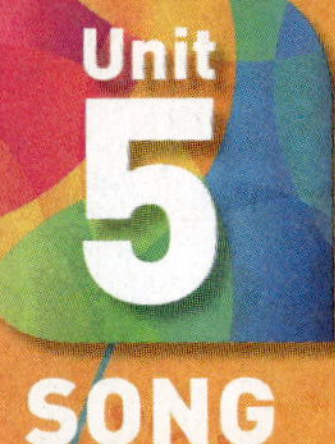

Unit 5
SONG

Celtic Alleluia

Music by Fintan O'Carroll

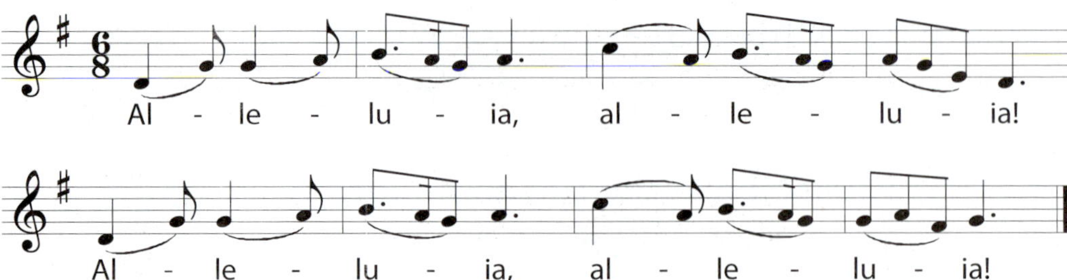

© 1985, GIA Publications, Inc.

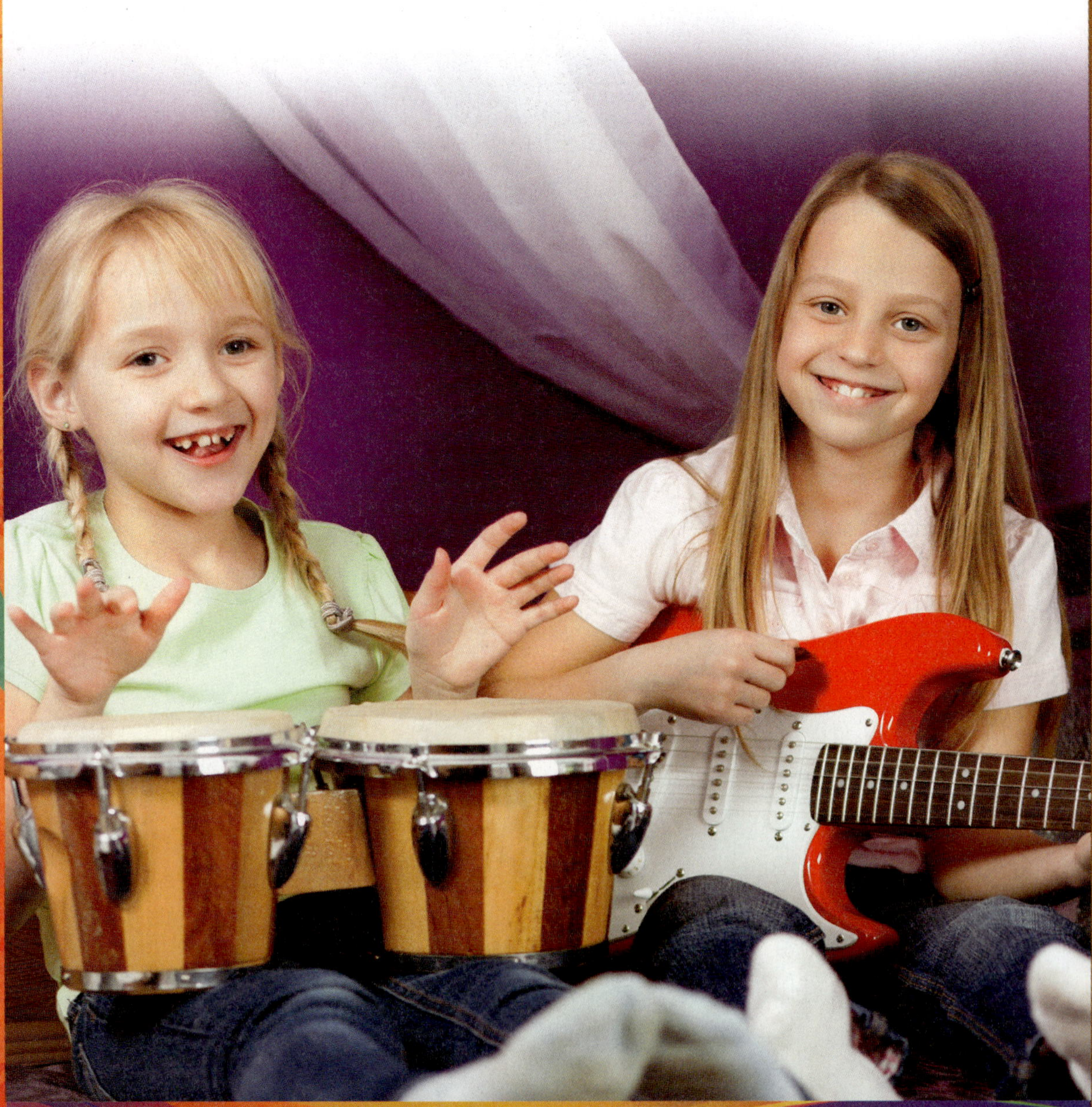

Getting ready for Chapter 17

Take Home

God Gives Us the Holy Spirit

In this chapter, the children will learn that the Holy Spirit is our helper, guide, and teacher. They will think about the spiritual gifts listed in Paul's first letter to the Corinthians.

ACTIVITY **Family Gift Night**

Have family members draw names and give a small present to one other family member. The gift should represent a talent the person has.

THROUGH THE WEEK

A PRAYER FOR THE WEEK Holy Spirit, thank you for the gifts of wisdom and knowledge. May we use them, as Saint Catherine of Siena did, to help others. Amen.

ON SUNDAY

Pray for the people who, in the name of the assembly, bring forward the gifts at the preparation of the altar and gifts.

ON THE WEB

BlestAreWe.com

RCLBLectionary.com

SaintsResource.com

Saint Catherine of Siena (1347–1380)

Catherine was the youngest of twenty-five children. At the age of six, she had a vision in which Jesus appeared and blessed her. At sixteen she became a Dominican sister. God gave Saint Catherine the gift of wisdom, which she used to give guidance to others.

Patron Saint of: firefighters, nurses, and sick people

Feast Day: April 29

Take Home

Scripture Background

In the Time of the Early Church

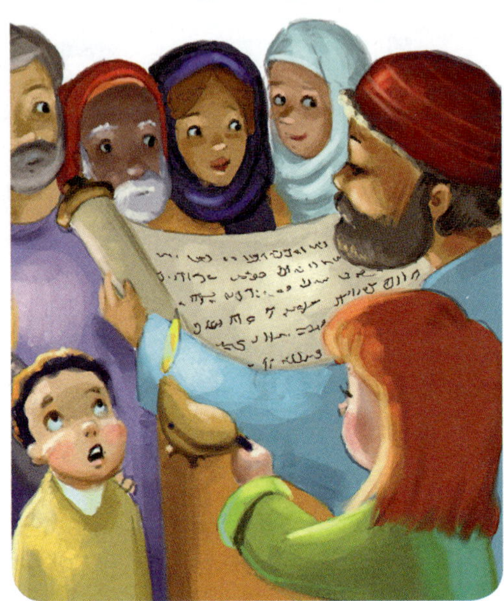

Corinth Corinth was a bustling seaport city in Greece. As such, it attracted people of various religions. Paul cherished the Christians living in Corinth, even though factions within the community caused him much frustration. In his first letter to them, Paul reminds the Corinthians of Jesus' message and the need for correct behavior in worship, a call for living peacefully, and living according to the power of true Christian love.

You can read of Paul's call for Christian unity in 1 Corinthians 12.

Our Catholic Tradition in Architecture

Hagia Sofia The Hagia Sofia, Greek for "holy wisdom," was built in the sixth century in Constantinople (now Istanbul, Turkey) by the emperor Justinian. The cathedral was named for the Gift of the Holy Spirit and remains one of the finest examples of Byzantine architecture.

After the Turks conquered Constantinople in the fifteenth century, the Hagia Sophia became a mosque, or Islamic house of worship. Its mosaics and Christian symbols were covered with plaster. The Hagia Sofia stayed that way until the twentieth century, when it became a museum and some of its original mosaics were uncovered.

God Gives Us the Holy Spirit

Chapter 17

. . . God sent the spirit of his Son into our hearts, . . .

Galatians 4:6

Share

All people have special gifts. We can use these gifts to help others.

Some people are smart. They help others learn.

Some people are funny. They cheer up people who are sad.

Some people are kind. They make life easier for others.

What is one special gift you have?

I can Have 2 toy.

How can you use this gift to help others?

What are spiritual gifts?

Hear and Believe **Scripture**

 The Spiritual Gifts

Some of Paul's friends lived in the city of Corinth. They asked Paul about the best way to serve God and their community. Paul wrote this letter to them.

Dear Friends,

God loves you very much. God sends you the Holy Spirit. The Holy Spirit helps you to live as good followers of Jesus.

The Holy Spirit gives us **spiritual gifts**. We use these gifts to help others and ourselves. Some of these gifts are wisdom, healing, knowledge, and faith. The Holy Spirit may give one person the gift of wisdom. He may give another person the gift of healing. To someone else, he may give knowledge or faith.

Show your love for God by sharing your gifts with each other. The Church community needs each person's gifts!

Peace and love,

Paul

Based on 1 Corinthians 12:4–11; 14:12

Gifts to Share

Paul's letter says that the Holy Spirit gives each of us spiritual gifts. Some gifts are knowledge, wisdom, healing, and faith. We use them to help others and ourselves. We use them to build up the Church.

Our Church Teaches

We receive the Holy Spirit in the Sacraments. The Holy Spirit is our helper, guide, and teacher. He helps us share our gifts with other people and with the Church. The Holy Spirit guides us in our daily lives.

We Believe

The Holy Spirit gives us spiritual gifts to share with others. These gifts help us follow Jesus.

Faith Words

spiritual gifts
Spiritual gifts are given to us by the Holy Spirit. We use them to help others and ourselves.

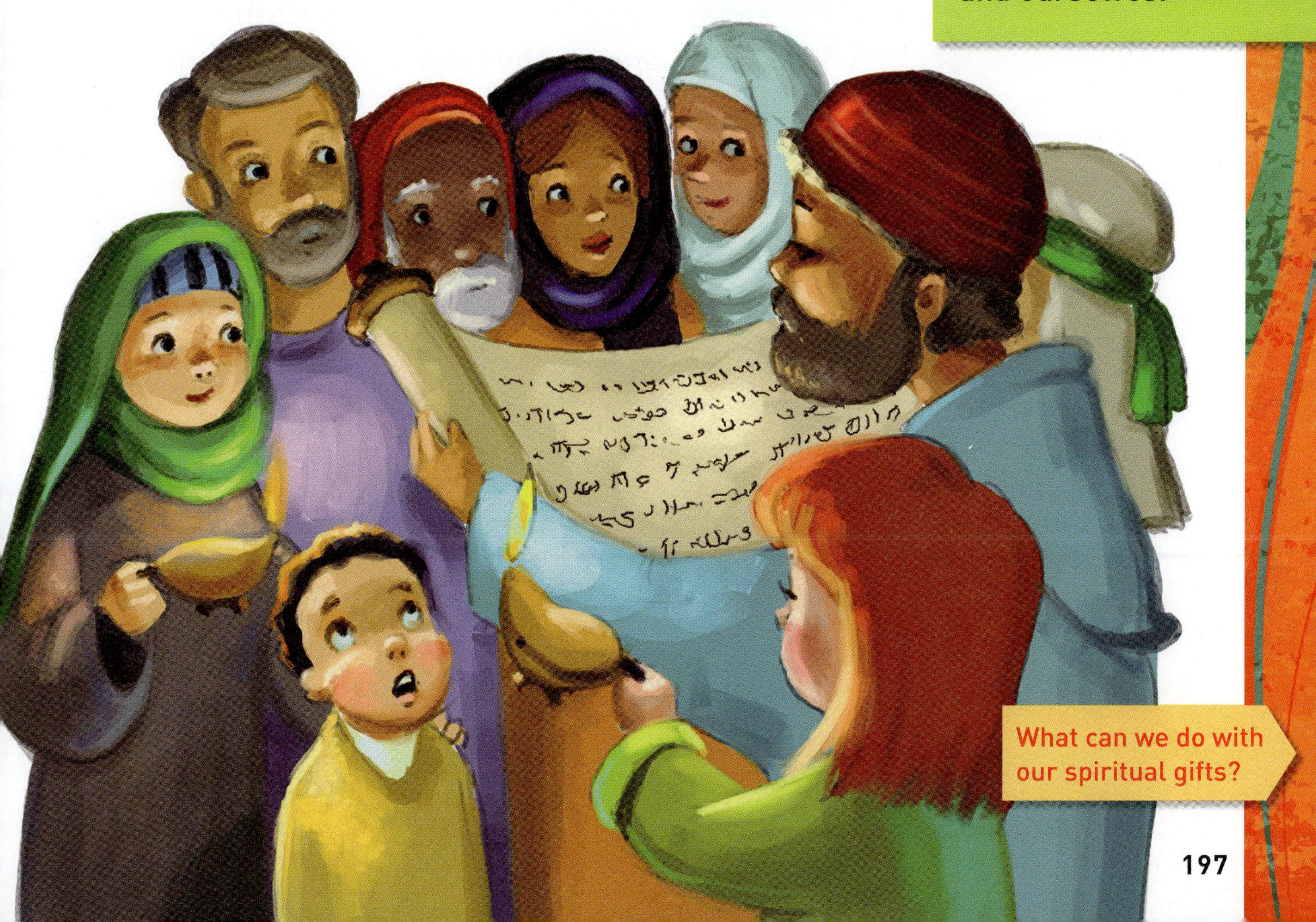

What can we do with our spiritual gifts?

Respond The Gift of Wisdom

In 2014, Pope Francis gave a special talk. It was about the gift of wisdom. He was not talking about wisdom that comes from reading a book. Pope Francis was talking about the gift of wisdom that comes from the Holy Spirit.

Pope Francis said that people who have this gift see with the eyes of God. They hear with God's ears. They love with God's heart. They obey God's laws. People with this gift grow in wisdom by praying. They listen to God's voice.

Pope Francis asked all Catholics to pray to the Holy Spirit for the gift of wisdom.

ACTIVITIES

1. Color the words on the banner. Then add a symbol of the Holy Spirit. Some symbols are a dove, flames, a lamp, rays of light, and a cloud.

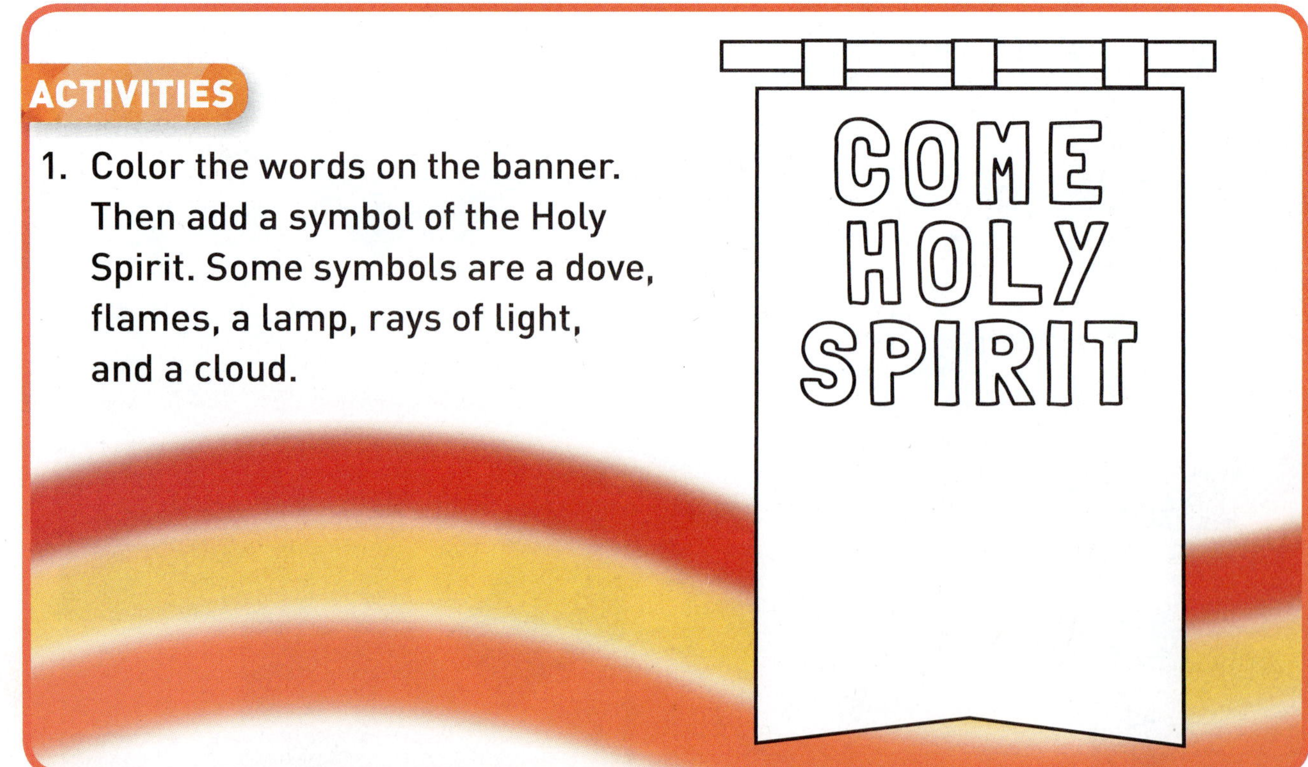

2. Pope Francis said that people who have the gift of wisdom love with God's heart.

Put a ✔ under Yes if the person is loving with God's heart.

Put a ✔ under No if the person is not loving with God's heart.

	YES	NO
a. Annie helps her mother fold clothes.	☐	☐
b. Jimmy throws his clothes on the floor.	☐	☐
c. Max tells lies about Sam.	☐	☐
d. Sara shares her lunch with a new student.	☐	☐
e. The Gomez family takes dinner to a neighbor who is sick.	☐	☐
f. The second graders take up a food collection for the poor.	☐	☐
g. Carlos makes fun of his baby brother.	☐	☐

How can we pray to the Holy Spirit?

A Prayer to the Holy Spirit

Leader: The Holy Spirit gives gifts to each person. These gifts are used to serve God and others. They are given to help the Church, the Body of Christ. Let us pray that we may always use our gifts to help others.

Leader: O God, send the Holy Spirit

Group 1: into our hearts that we may love,

Group 2: into our minds that we may remember,

Group 3: into our imaginations that we may understand.

Leader: May the grace of the Holy Spirit strengthen us with wisdom.

All: **May the Holy Spirit help and guide us. Amen.**

Based on the Holy Spirit Prayer of Saint Anthony of Padua

Chapter Review 17

A **Write** about what the Holy Spirit wants us to do with our spiritual gifts.

____

____

B **Circle** the word that best completes each sentence.

1. The Church needs the ______ of each person.

   belongings gifts pictures

2. The Holy Spirit is our helper, guide, and ______.

   parent priest teacher

3. God wants us to open our ______ to the Holy Spirit.

   books desks hearts

4. Knowledge, wisdom, and faith are ______ gifts from the Holy Spirit.

   expensive song spiritual

5. Spiritual gifts help us to follow ______.

   angels Jesus strangers

Faith in Action

Pastoral Assistants Pastoral assistants bring together the work of all parish ministers. They might plan liturgy, visit the sick, or work in the parish office. Pastoral assistants work with priests, deacons, and other leaders in the parish.

In Everyday Life

ACTIVITY The sentences below tell about leaders and the people they lead. Circle the word that best completes each sentence.

- Coaches lead **players students** on a team.
- Parents lead their **children classmates** to grow in their faith.

Now complete this sentence.

Children lead their ____________________ to make good decisions.

In Your Parish

ACTIVITY Think about all the people you see who lead activities in your parish. What Gifts of the Holy Spirit do you see being used to serve your parish?

____

____

Take Home

We Celebrate Peace and Service

The children will learn that we greet each other at Mass by offering those around us the Sign of Peace. This sign reminds us that Jesus wants us to get along with everyone and to serve one another.

ACTIVITY **Helping Hands**

Invite family members to trace their hands on colored paper. On the hands, write ways you can help others. Display the "helping hands" as a reminder to do so.

THROUGH THE WEEK

A PRAYER FOR THE WEEK O God, may we always be willing to serve you and your people. Help us to see your presence in everyone we meet. May we follow the example of Saint Anthony of Padua. Amen.

ON SUNDAY
As you share the Sign of Peace at Mass, think about how you can make peace in your family.

ON THE WEB
BlestAreWe.com
RCLBLectionary.com
SaintsResource.com

Saint Anthony of Padua (1195–1231)

Anthony of Padua was a Franciscan friar. He preached and taught men who were training to be priests. He also helped people who felt lost and confused. Saint Anthony was canonized in 1232. In 1946 he was named a Doctor of the Church.

Patron Saint of: animals, seekers of lost articles

Feast Day: June 13

Take Home

Scripture Background

In the Time of the Early Church

Agape The Greek word *agape* means "love." In the New Testament, it designates the unmerited love God shows to humankind by sending Jesus as our suffering Redeemer. The word is also used to describe a fellowship meal following the celebration of the Eucharist. When applied to human love, *agape* means "selfless love."

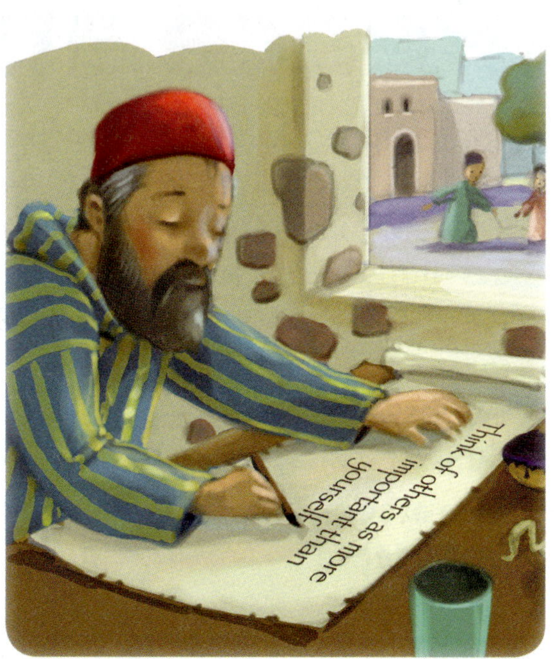

You can read about Paul's description of true Christian love in 1 Corinthians 13.

Our Catholic Tradition

in Religious Life

Saint Jeanne Jugan Saint Jeanne Jugan, also known as Sister Mary of the Cross (1792–1879), grew up as a poor French girl. From her youth she felt that she was called to do something special. In 1839, Jeanne formed a community of prayer and good works. From that small beginning, she established an order called the Little Sisters of the Poor, whose mission is to care for the elderly in need. In addition to the vows of poverty, chastity, and obedience, this group takes a vow of hospitality. In October of 2009, Jeanne Jugan was canonized by Pope Benedict XVI. Today, there are Little Sisters of the Poor in more than thirty countries on five continents.

We Celebrate Peace and Service

Chapter 18

. . . [G]race to you and peace from God our Father and the Lord Jesus Christ. 2 Corinthians 1:2

Share

We greet other people with words or with actions.

The people in the pictures want to say "Hello." Each of them wants to say it in a different way. Write a different greeting below for each person.

How do we greet each other at Mass?

The Sign of Peace

At each Mass, we offer those around us the Sign of Peace. Peace is a sign that the Holy Spirit is with us. The Sign of Peace reminds us that Jesus wants us to get along with everyone. It reminds us that we are to serve one another each day.

We share the Sign of Peace in this way:

Priest: Lord Jesus Christ,
who said to your Apostles:
Peace I leave you, my peace I give you,
look not on our sins,
but on the faith of your Church,
and graciously grant her peace and unity
in accordance with your will.
Who live and reign for ever and ever.

All: **Amen.**

Priest: The peace of the Lord be with you always.

All: **And with your spirit.**

Priest: Let us offer each other the sign of peace.

Roman Missal

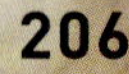

We Are Called to Serve

The Sign of Peace reminds us that Jesus wants us to love one another. Jesus wants us to live together in peace. The Sign of Peace calls all members of the Church to serve one another. We can do this by taking part in parish activities.

Our Church Teaches

There are different ways of serving others. Some men are called to serve as priests, deacons, or bishops. They receive the Sacrament of **Holy Orders**. Some men and women are called to work for the good of others by being married. They celebrate the Sacrament of **Matrimony**.

Holy Orders and Matrimony are Sacraments at the Service of Communion. Baptized men who receive Holy Orders teach and serve others. In Matrimony, a baptized man and a baptized woman promise to be faithful to each other as husband and wife. Married people share their love by loving and caring for their children. People who receive these Sacraments serve the People of God, the Church.

We Believe

Holy Orders and Matrimony are Sacraments at the Service of Communion.

Faith Words

Holy Orders
In the Sacrament of Holy Orders, bishops, priests, and deacons are ordained to special service in the Church.

Matrimony
In the Sacrament of Matrimony, a baptized man and a baptized woman promise to be faithful to each other for their whole lives.

In what way can we celebrate our call to service?

Respond Called to Serve

The pope is the leader of the Church all over the world. He has the same job in the Church that Jesus gave to Saint Peter.

The word *pope* comes from a Latin word that means "papa." The pope is sometimes called the Holy Father.

Pope Francis became pope in 2013. Cardinal Jorge Bergoglio chose the name Francis after he was elected pope. He chose the name to honor Saint Francis of Assisi. He is the first pope to come from Latin America. He grew up in Argentina and became a Jesuit priest. Pope John Paul II named him a cardinal in 2001.

One of the main jobs of the pope is to appoint a bishop for each diocese. A diocese is the Church in a particular part of the world.

Your bishop, and all the other bishops, work together with the pope to lead and serve the Church. They help the Church grow in holiness. They help us live as faithful disciples of Jesus.

How does the pope act as a faithful disciple of Jesus?

ACTIVITIES

1. Color each space that has a cross. Write the hidden message on the line below the picture. Then color the picture.

2. Show the way Pope Francis grew in his vocation. Put the following terms in order. Number them from 1 to 3.

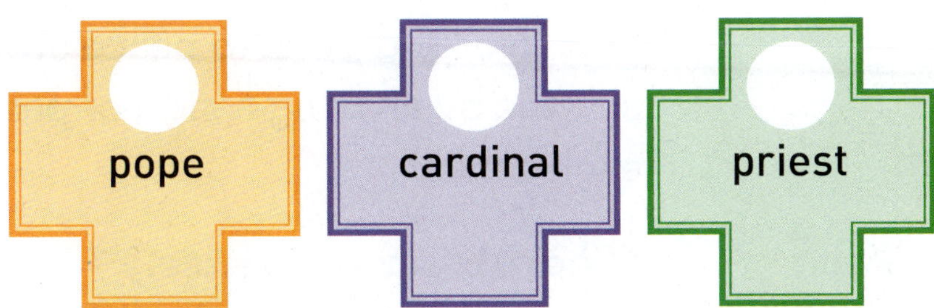

In what ways can we celebrate people who serve others?

A Prayer of Thanks

Leader: O God, you call us to live in peace and to serve others. We give thanks for Matrimony and Holy Orders, the Sacraments at the Service of Communion.

Reader 1: Holy Spirit of love, we celebrate our parents who teach us about our faith.

All: **Thank you, God, for the gift of our parents.**

Reader 2: Holy Spirit of kindness, we celebrate the priests and deacons in our parish who serve us.

All: **Thank you, God, for the gift of people who serve.**

Reader 3: Holy Spirit of peace, we celebrate the many kinds of families in our parish.

All: **Thank you, God, for the gift of each other.**

Leader: Let us follow the example of those who live God's call to peace and service by sharing a sign of peace with each other.

All: ***(Share a sign of peace.)***

Chapter Review 18

A **Draw a line** to connect the parts of each sentence.

1. We are to work for the ______ of others. •	• good
2. Deacons, priests, and bishops receive the Sacrament of ______. •	• get along
3. In Matrimony, a baptized man and a baptized woman promise to be faithful to ______. •	• Holy Orders
4. The Sign of Peace reminds us that Jesus wants us to ______ with everyone. •	• each other

B **Complete** the sentences with words from the box.

People	Matrimony	caring

1. A baptized man and woman receive the Sacrament of ______________________.

2. Deacons, priests, and bishops teach and serve the ______________________ of God.

3. Married people share their love by loving and ______________________ for their children.

Faith in Action

Ministers of Hospitality At church, some people serve as ministers of hospitality. They welcome people. They help people find seats at Mass. They collect money offerings. They have many other responsibilities.

In Everyday Life

ACTIVITY Think about how people in your family serve each other. Name two ways you can serve family members.

____

____

In Your Parish

ACTIVITY Color the boxes yellow that show service at church. Color green the ones that are not service.

- opening a door just for yourself
- helping carry groceries
- making thank-you cards
- putting away song books

Getting ready for Chapter 19

Take Home

We Work for Peace and Justice

In Chapter 19 the children will consider the concepts of peace and justice and identify actions they can take to promote these concepts. The children will realize that Jesus taught us to treat others fairly and respectfully.

ACTIVITY **Certificate of Fairness**

With your child, make a simple certificate with the words "Fairness Counts" at the top. Add words associated with fairness, such as sharing, helping, and giving. Each time your child acts fairly this week, give her or him a sticker to add to the certificate.

THROUGH THE WEEK

A PRAYER FOR THE WEEK Lord, you call upon us to speak up for what is true and just. May we have the courage to work for peace and justice as did Saint Catherine of Alexandria. Amen.

ON SUNDAY

Other than in the Sign of Peace, when is peace mentioned in the liturgy? Listen for other mentions of peace in the prayers, readings, and hymns of the Mass.

ON THE WEB

BlestAreWe.com

RCLBLectionary.com

SaintsResource.com

Saint Catherine of Alexandria (d. 305)

Catherine of Alexandria lived in Africa. She was an intelligent woman who opposed evil and lived a life of truth and justice. After challenging the pagan emperor she was martyred for her faith.

Patron Saint of: craftspeople, scholars, and students

Feast Day: November 25

Take Home

Scripture Background
In the Time of the Early Church

First Christian Community The Apostle Peter established the Church in Jerusalem. Christians there tried to adhere to the teachings of the Apostles and to make the celebration of the Eucharist the center of their religious life. Through a system of fair distribution, the wealthy sold their possessions for the needs of the poor. At the time, followers of Jesus continued the practice of worshiping in the Temple as Jews.

You can read of the communal life of the Christians in Acts 2:42–47, 4:32–37.

Our Catholic Tradition in Volunteerism

Catholic Network of Volunteer Service

The non-profit organization Catholic Network of Volunteer Service (CNVS) was formed in 1963. Its goal is to help women and men use their gifts by volunteering service to others. Special programs help connect volunteers with volunteer opportunities. CNVS supports community-based programs, such as AmeriCorps, which is the domestic Peace Corps. AmeriCorps encourages youth to help other youth overcome illiteracy, poverty, crime, and homelessness, and also addresses environmental problems. Learn more about the Catholic Network of Volunteer Service at cnvs.org, and more about the work of AmeriCorps at nationalservice.gov.

We Work for Peace and Justice

Chapter 19

"Blessed are the peacemakers, for they will be called children of God." Matthew 5:9

Share

When we are home or at school, we want to be treated fairly. When we are at church or in our community, we work to treat others fairly.

She shares.

☐ fair ☐ unfair

ACTIVITY

Look at the pictures. Use a ✔ to mark each one fair or unfair.

He steals.

☐ fair ☐ unfair

She helps.

☐ fair ☐ unfair

He gives.

☐ fair ☐ unfair

She peeks.

☐ fair ☐ unfair

In what ways does Jesus want us to act?

Hear and Believe Scripture

The First Followers of Jesus

The first followers of Jesus tried to treat everyone fairly. If life was difficult, they tried to help make it better. Here is how the early Christians treated one another.

The Christians were all of one heart and one mind.
They tried to make peace and they tried to be kind.
They shared what they had, both the rich
and the poor,
So no one went hungry or wanted for more.
Those who had extra would sell what they had.
They took care of those who were sick or were sad.
If someone was needy, other Christians came.
They brought food or money in Christ Jesus' name.

Based on Acts 4:32–35

What Jesus Taught

Jesus taught us to live in **peace**. When there is fighting, Christians try to make peace. Jesus also taught us to treat everyone fairly, with **justice**. We comfort people who need extra help. We share with people who have less.

Our Church Teaches

We are to treat people the way we want to be treated. We grow in holiness when we make peace and treat others fairly. The Holy Spirit helps us to live as faithful members of our Church.

We Believe

We follow Jesus when we do what is right. Christians believe that all people deserve to be treated justly.

Faith Words

peace
Peace means getting along with others.

justice
Justice means treating people fairly.

In what ways can we make peace and act with justice?

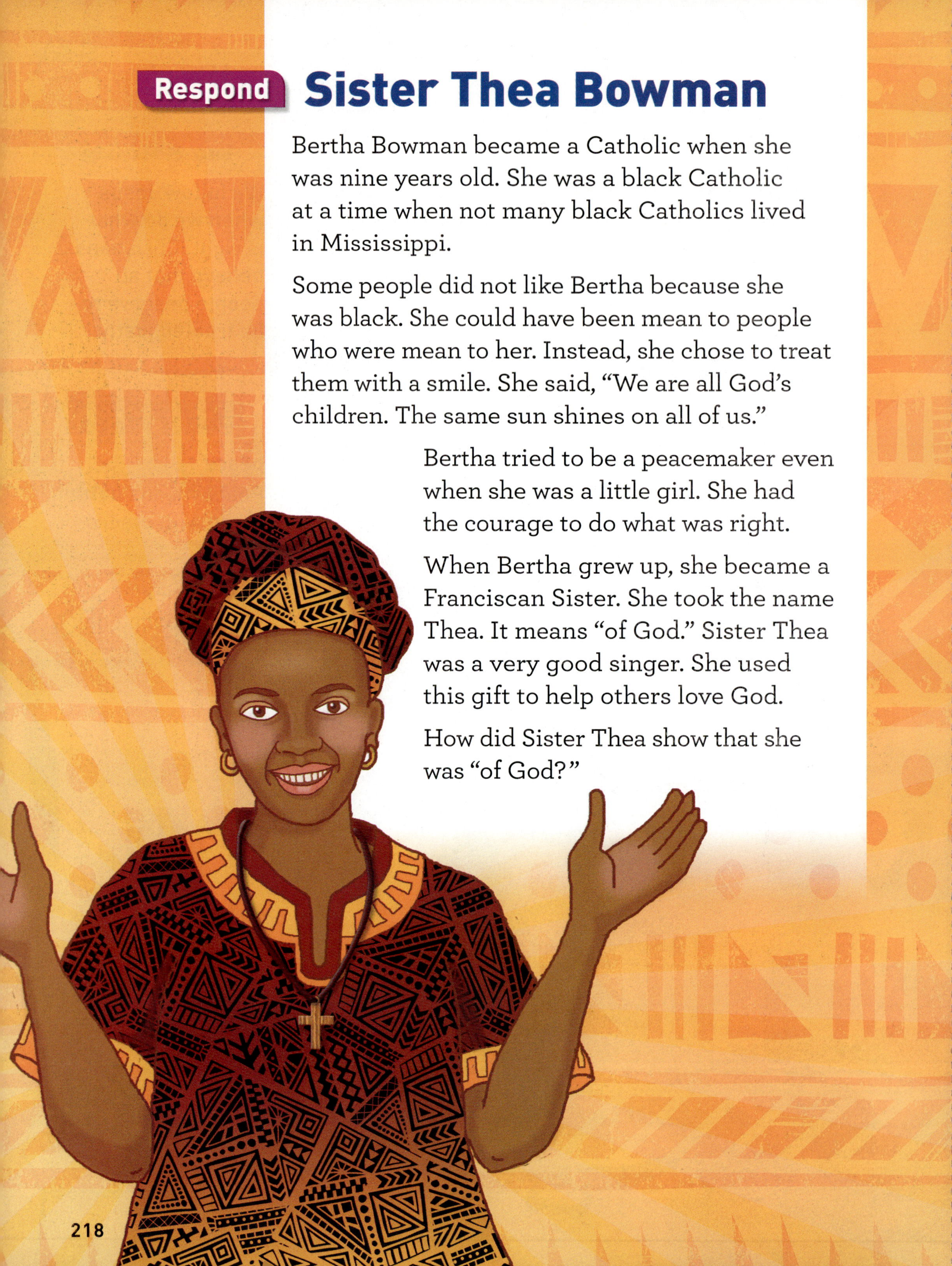

Respond Sister Thea Bowman

Bertha Bowman became a Catholic when she was nine years old. She was a black Catholic at a time when not many black Catholics lived in Mississippi.

Some people did not like Bertha because she was black. She could have been mean to people who were mean to her. Instead, she chose to treat them with a smile. She said, "We are all God's children. The same sun shines on all of us."

Bertha tried to be a peacemaker even when she was a little girl. She had the courage to do what was right.

When Bertha grew up, she became a Franciscan Sister. She took the name Thea. It means "of God." Sister Thea was a very good singer. She used this gift to help others love God.

How did Sister Thea show that she was "of God?"

ACTIVITY

Jesus said, "Blessed are the peacemakers, for they will be called children of God" (based on Matthew 5:9). Sister Thea Bowman lived Jesus' message. Learn to sign Jesus' words so you will remember to follow them.

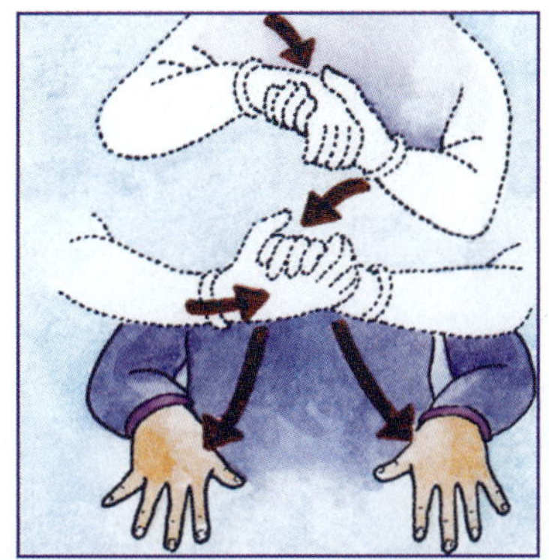

Blessed (are the) peacemakers, (for)

they will be called

children (of) God.

In what ways can we celebrate God's gifts of peace and justice?

A Signing Prayer

Leader: O God, we ask you to bless those who work for peace and justice. We pray for all people who try to stop wars and make peace.

All: **(*Sign:* Blessed are the peacemakers.)**

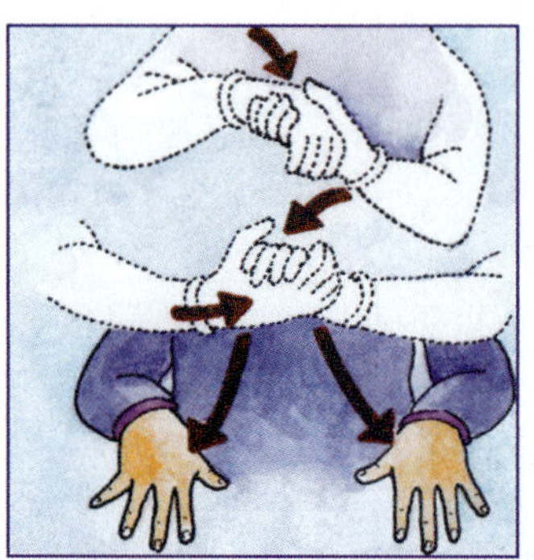

Blessed (are the) peacemakers.

Leader: Jesus, bless those who try to be like you and treat people in need with justice.

All: **(*Sign:* Blessed are the peacemakers.)**

Leader: Holy Spirit, we ask that you help us live in peace and work for justice.

All: **(*Sign:* Blessed are the peacemakers.)**

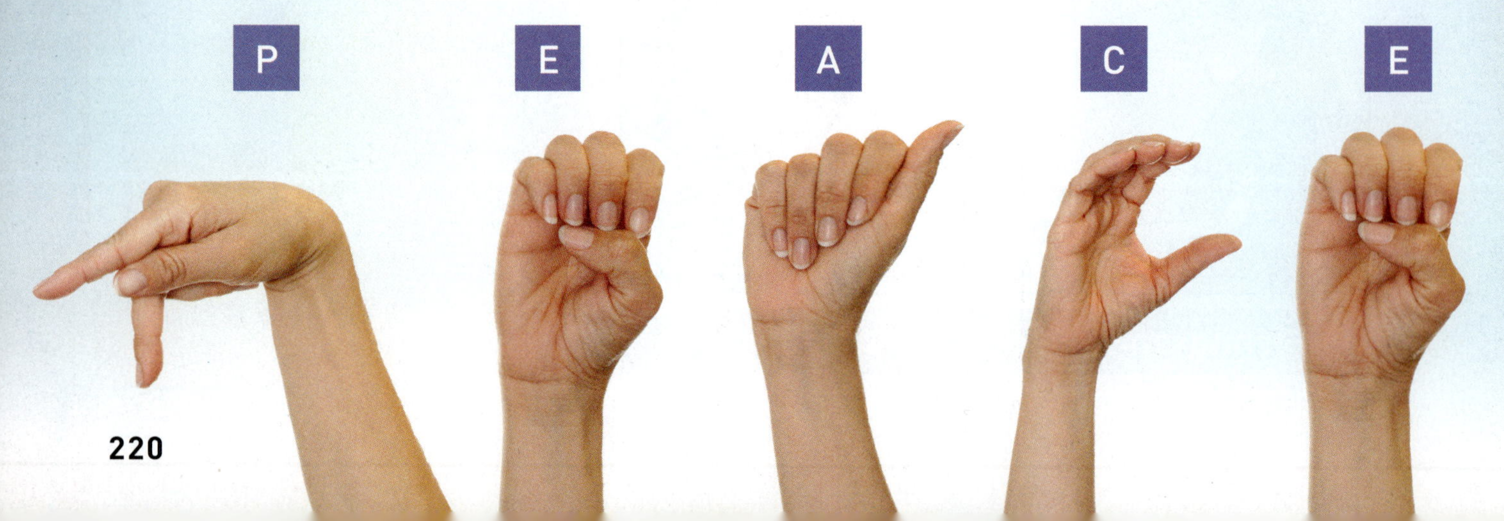

Chapter Review 19

A **Write or draw** one way to make peace with someone.

B **Circle** the words that best complete the sentences.

1. Christians try to make ______.

   money   peace   food

2. ______ means "getting along with others."

   Peace   Justice   Healthy

3. ______ is fair treatment for everyone.

   Peace   Justice   Stealing

4. We grow in ______ when we make peace.

   age   fear   holiness

5. Jesus said, "______ are the peacemakers."

   Blessed   Tired   Worried

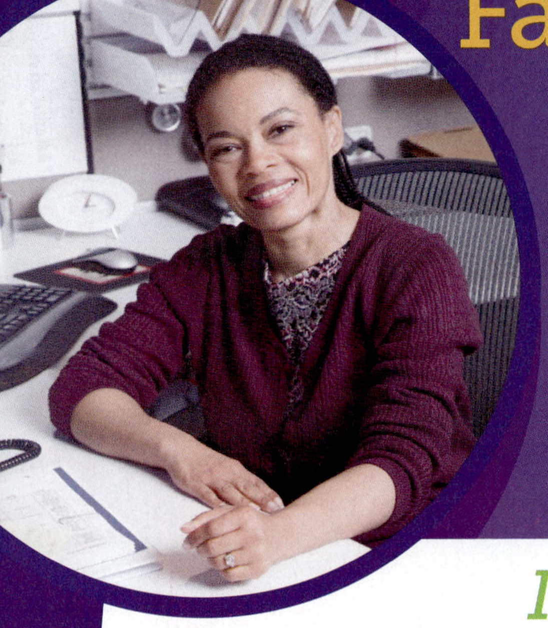

Faith in Action

Parish Staff In addition to your parish priests and deacons, office assistants, janitors, groundskeepers, and so on, all have special jobs that help keep the parish running smoothly. They all use their gifts to serve others.

In Everyday Life

ACTIVITY **Draw a line** from each worker to what that worker does.

a. crossing guard •	• helps us be healthy
b. bus driver •	• helps us learn new things
c. doctor •	• brings us letters
d. mail carrier •	• helps us cross streets safely
e. teacher •	• gets us places we want to go

What work will you do when you grow up?
How will you serve others?

In Your Parish

ACTIVITY Think about the work that someone at your parish does. Write down that person's name and what he or she does.

____

____

Getting ready for Chapter 20

Take Home

We Go Forth in the Holy Spirit

We bless God when we praise and thank him, and we can pray to God to bless others. In Chapter 20 the children will learn that blessings are signs of God's love. They will write prayers of blessing.

ACTIVITY **Bless Our Home**

With your child, write a prayer that asks for God's blessing on each person in your family, on the activities of your family members, and on your home.

THROUGH THE WEEK

A PRAYER FOR THE WEEK O God, thank you for the many blessings you give us. May we follow the example of Saint Rose Philippine Duchesne and be willing to bless others. Amen.

ON SUNDAY

At the end of Mass the priest or deacon says, "Go in peace, glorifying the Lord by your life." Think of one way to do that in the coming week.

ON THE WEB

BlestAreWe.com

RCLBLectionary.com

SaintsResource.com

Saint Rose Philippine Duchesne (1769–1852)

Mother Duchesne was a sister in the Society of the Sacred Heart in France. She traveled to the Louisiana Territory as a missionary and opened schools for children of pioneers and Native American people.

Patron Saint of: Native Americans

Feast Day: November 18

Take Home

Scripture Background

Before the Time of Jesus

Blessings The first Old Testament blessing is described in Genesis 1:28. After creating humankind, God said, "Be fertile and multiply." This is also called a *benediction*, which means "blessing." Common blessings involve fertility, health, longevity, the satisfying of needs, and a generally happy life. Jesus carried on the ritual of giving blessings during his earthly life.

You can read about the first blessing in Genesis 1:24–31.

Our Catholic Tradition in Architecture

Church of the Beatitudes In the place where Jesus spoke the Beatitudes to his followers, there is a church that is named after them. The Church of the Beatitudes is located along the northern shore of the Sea of Galilee on the mount near Capernaum, home to five of Jesus' Twelve Apostles. Built in 1937, the church is octagonal to represent the eight Beatitudes that Matthew describes in his Gospel (see Matthew 5:3–10). Inscribed on each window are the beginning words of one of the Beatitudes. A dome of gold mosaic covers the altar and rests on top of the building. Surrounding the outside of the church are columned cloisters. These provide a panoramic view of the Sea of Galilee.

We Go Forth in the Holy Spirit

Chapter 20

May the LORD give might to his people;
may the LORD bless his people with peace! Psalm 29:11

Share

God's gifts are all around us. These gifts make us happy. We receive God's gifts through our five senses. Think about the good things that have happened to you this year. Write about them here.

Something beautiful I saw

____

Something wonderful I heard

____

Something nice I smelled

____

Something good I tasted

____

Something soft I touched

____

In what ways can we praise God and bless other people?

Hear and Believe Scripture

God's Grace and Blessing

God spoke to Moses one day. God said, "Moses, speak to your brother Aaron and his sons. Tell them how to bless others."

"All right," Moses answered. Then Moses told Aaron and his sons, "God wants you to **bless** people. Pray for them and say,

'May God bless you and keep you safe!
May God smile upon you!
May God look upon you kindly!
May God always give you peace!'"

Based on Numbers 6:22–26

Scripture Verse
The LORD bless
you and keep you!
Numbers 6:24

Signs of God's Love

A **blessing** is a sign of God's love for us. God told Moses how to give blessings to other people. The Holy Spirit helps us offer prayers of blessing to God. We bless God when we give praise and thanks for his many gifts.

Our Church Teaches

When we bless God, we give him thanks and praise. We ask God to bless others. We ask that he fill others with love and peace. We ask God to bless us. We ask for God's help through the Holy Spirit.

We Believe

God gives everyone many blessings. We bless God with thanks and praise. We ask God to bless all people.

Faith Words

bless
To bless means to ask for God's good will toward someone.

blessing
A blessing asks for God's gifts for others or for ourselves. It is a sign of God's love.

In what ways can we share our blessings with others?

Respond We Love and Serve

Each Mass ends with a blessing. The priest asks God to bless us. He reminds us to carry on the work of Jesus. We do this by helping, caring for, and serving others.

Priest: May almighty God bless you, the Father, and the Son, and the Holy Spirit.

All: **Amen.**

Priest: Go in peace, glorifying the Lord by your life.

All: **Thanks be to God.**

The Concluding Rites, *Roman Missal*

Ways To Glorify The Lord By Loving And Serving Others

We can be kind and patient.

We can cheerfully do chores and homework.

We can try to be helpful.

We can care for plants and animals.

We can share.

We can take part in parish activities.

We can ask God to bless others.

How will you love and serve others this week?

ACTIVITIES

1. Find and circle six words about ways to love and serve others. Use words from the box.

C	H	E	E	R	F	U	L	P
X	E	L	C	Y	K	B	D	A
B	L	R	S	S	O	N	C	T
L	P	C	H	O	N	V	L	I
E	F	E	A	Z	D	I	W	E
S	U	D	R	R	O	O	V	N
S	L	G	E	M	E	P	S	T

bless

care

cheerful

helpful

patient

share

2. Write a prayer of blessing for someone you know.

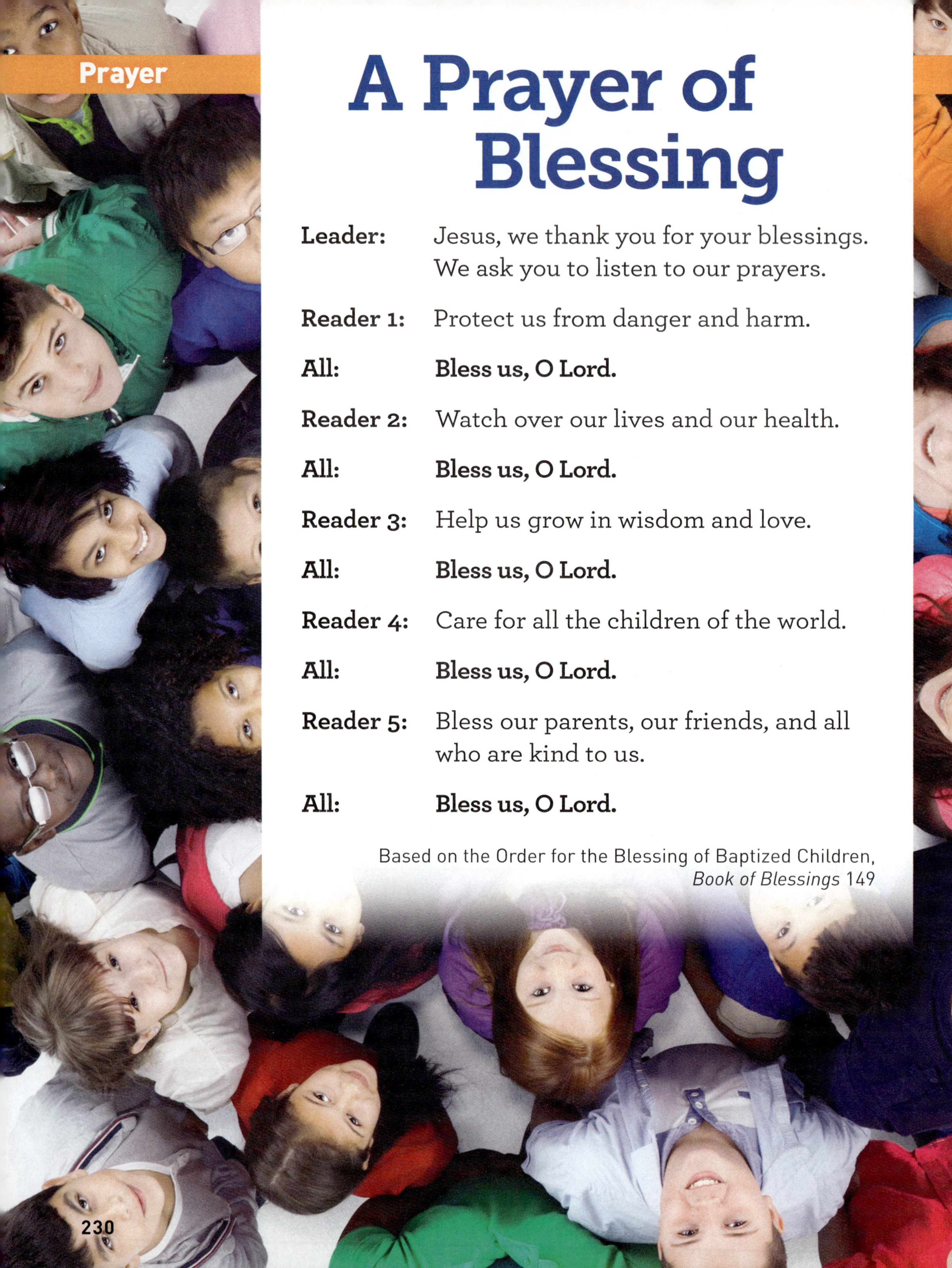

A Prayer of Blessing

Leader: Jesus, we thank you for your blessings. We ask you to listen to our prayers.

Reader 1: Protect us from danger and harm.

All: **Bless us, O Lord.**

Reader 2: Watch over our lives and our health.

All: **Bless us, O Lord.**

Reader 3: Help us grow in wisdom and love.

All: **Bless us, O Lord.**

Reader 4: Care for all the children of the world.

All: **Bless us, O Lord.**

Reader 5: Bless our parents, our friends, and all who are kind to us.

All: **Bless us, O Lord.**

Based on the Order for the Blessing of Baptized Children, *Book of Blessings* 149

Chapter Review 20

A **Circle** the best answer.

1. Which word means "to ask for God's good will?"

   bless　　care　　grace

2. What did God tell Moses to give to other people?

   gifts　　maps　　blessings

3. To whom does God give blessings?

   priests　　the pope　　everyone

4. What is a blessing a sign of?

   hate　　love　　summer

5. Who helps us give prayers of blessing to God?

   Adam　　the Holy Spirit　　Moses

B **Write** on each line the letter for the word that best completes the sentence.

A. love	B. help	C. peace	D. praise

1. Moses told Aaron to say, "May God always give you ______."
2. When we ask God to bless others, we ask him to fill them with ______ and peace.
3. When we bless God, we give thanks and ______ to God.
4. We ask for God's ______ through the Holy Spirit.

Faith in Action

Sharing With Others Children of every age can share what they have with others who have less. They can collect used books or clothing. They can collect canned food and money for parish and community outreach ministries.

In Everyday Life

ACTIVITY Do you have good clothes that don't fit anymore? Do you have toys or games that you don't use? List things you have that you could share with children in need. Take time this week to gather some of these things to donate to help others in need.

Things I Can Donate

In Your Parish

ACTIVITY With a partner, look through your parish bulletin to see the many ways your parish helps people in need. Talk about ways your religion class can help others in need, too. Share your ideas with your religion class.

Feasts and Seasons

Catholics celebrate seasons of the Church year. Each Sunday begins a special week. There are six seasons. Each one has its own symbols and colors.

Holy Week is not a season, but it is a very important week. It begins with Palm Sunday. It ends on Holy Thursday evening.

Holy Week leads us to the shortest season of the Church year. It is called the **Triduum**. We think about Jesus sharing the Last Supper with his Apostles, dying on the Cross, and rising to new life.

HOLY WEEK

The Church year begins.

ADVENT

Our Church year begins with **Advent**. For four weeks we prepare to celebrate the birth of Jesus.

ORDINARY TIME

In the second part of **Ordinary Time**, we learn more about the life and teachings of Jesus. This is the longest part of the Church year.

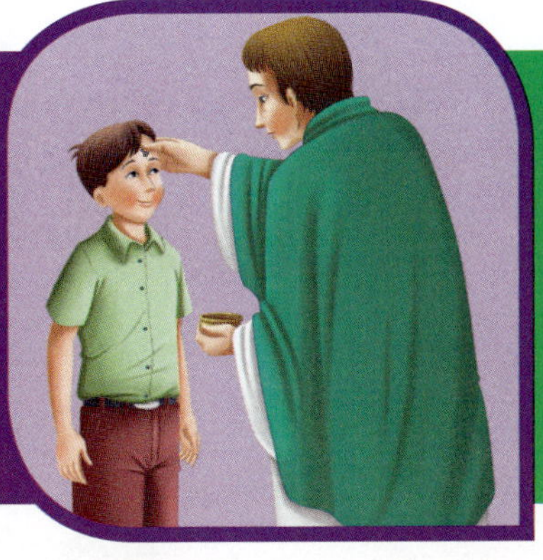

EASTER

Easter celebrates Jesus' Resurrection. It is a season of joy. It lasts fifty days until Pentecost Sunday. Then we celebrate the coming of the Holy Spirit.

LENT AND HOLY WEEK

The season of **Lent** lasts forty days. It begins with Ash Wednesday. We prepare for Easter through prayer and good works for others.

ORDINARY TIME

This part of **Ordinary Time** tells how Jesus began his work for people.

CHRISTMAS

At **Christmas** we celebrate the birth of Jesus. It is a season of gift giving and joy.

Sundays and Feast Days

Sunday is our greatest holy day. Sundays are important days to celebrate our Catholic faith.

We come together at Mass to celebrate Jesus' Resurrection. We celebrate the Eucharist with our parish. It is good to come together with our Church community.

Sunday also is a day to be happy, to rest, and to enjoy being with our families.

We celebrate many feast days during the Church year. Some of them are on Sunday. They honor Jesus, Mary, and the saints. These feast days help us grow in our faith.

Ordinary Time

 Seek first the Kingdom of God.

Based on Matthew 6:33

Special Church Objects

Special objects help us to pray in church.

Match each object with the sentence that tells about it. Put the matching letter in the correct box.

D  B  G  E

A  F  C

☐ **tabernacle**

☐ **altar**

☐ **crucifix**

☐ **Statue**

☐ **baptismal font**

☐ **Easter candle**

☐ **ambo**

A Special Season

Ordinary Time is the longest season of the Church year. It has two parts. The first part comes between Christmas and Lent. The second part comes between Easter and Advent.

Each week we go to Mass and listen to a Gospel reading. The Gospel stories during Ordinary Time tell us about Jesus' life on Earth. They help us know how to love God and our neighbor. At Mass we listen to the Gospels of Matthew, Mark, Luke, or John. They tell us the Good News of Jesus.

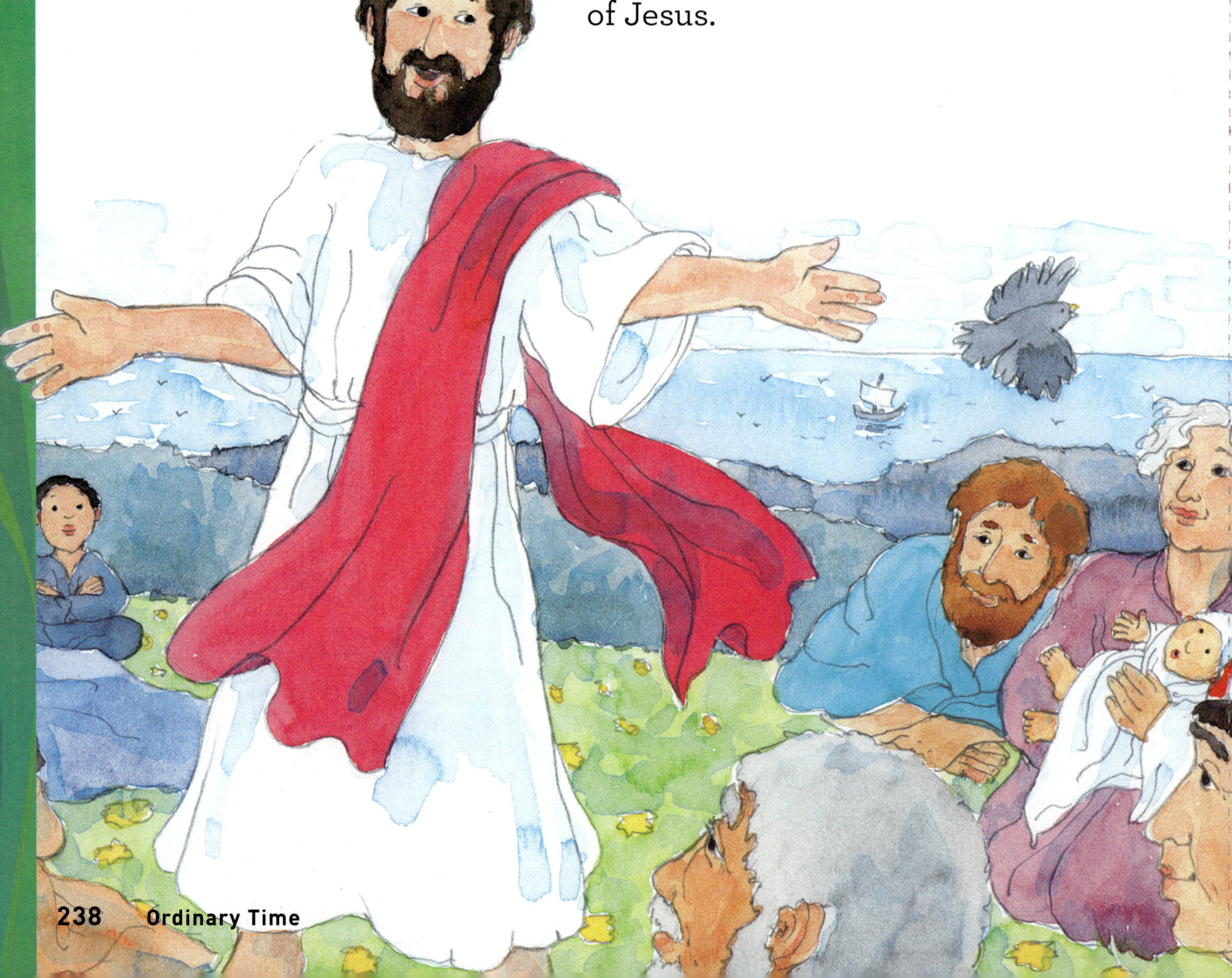

Solemnity of All Saints

People will know that you are my friends, if you love one another.

Based on John 13:35

What's in a Name?

Every person has a name that is special to him or her.

Our names identify us. Our names tell some interesting things about us.

ACTIVITY

What is your first name?

____

Why did your parents give you that name?

Check (✓) the reasons below that are true for you.

_____ I was given the same name as my mom or dad and am proud to have it.

_____ I was given my name to honor my grandparent or another family member.

_____ I was named after a favorite saint.

_____ My parents really loved my name and wanted me to have it.

_____ I was given the name of an outstanding person in my community or country.

Jovito

GISELA

Roger

Siok-Tin

Thomas

Chiara

All Saints

All holy women and men, pray for us that we may live more like Jesus. Amen.

Among Catholics it has long been a custom for parents to name their children for saints. Saints are people who live outstanding lives as followers of Jesus. Saints put all their energy into doing what is good. They work hard to overcome what is bad or wrong and to bring good to the world.

Francis of Assisi is one saint whom we honor. He gave up money, parties, and fancy clothes. Instead he spent his time in prayer, helping the poor, and caring for all of God's creatures.

Followers of Jesus

The Church names many people as saints. Each saint can help us learn more about how to be true followers of Jesus. In prayer we can ask the saints for help to lead good Christian lives. We can ask in prayer for fairness to all people and for peace among people.

We celebrate the Solemnity of All Saints on November 1.

Advent

... "Are you the one who is to come, or should we look for another?" Matthew 11:3

Preparing Our Hearts

Advent is the first season in the Church year. During Advent we get ready for Jesus to come into our lives. We prepare our hearts for Jesus. We remember to love and care for others.

ACTIVITY This Advent house has windows with messages written on them. Each message tells one way we can prepare our hearts to welcome Jesus.

For each week of Advent, choose one window and follow its message.

Help a neighbor or a family member with a chore.

Give time or money to help someone in need.

Welcome a newcomer to your church or school.

Pray for someone who is unhappy.

What else will you do during Advent to remember the birth of Jesus?

Waiting for the Promised One

One Advent reading at Mass tells the story of John the Baptist. He was a cousin of Jesus. John preached to people in the desert. He had a special message. He said,

> **". . . 'Prepare the way of the Lord, make straight his paths.'"**
>
> Matthew 3:3

Jesus, help us to care for others as we prepare to celebrate your birth. Amen.

He wanted the people to prepare their hearts and minds for Jesus.

> **When Jesus began teaching, John sent messengers to ask Jesus, "Are you the one for whom the people have been waiting for thousands of years?" Jesus answered, "Tell John that the blind see, the lame walk, the deaf hear, and the poor have heard the good news."**
>
> *Based on* Matthew 11:2–5

Hearing these words, John knew that Jesus was the Savior. The time of waiting was over.

Christmas

The shepherds hurried to Bethlehem, where they found Mary and Joseph, and the infant Jesus. *Based on* Luke 2:16

Jesus, we thank you for coming to be with us. Amen.

The Birth of Jesus

During the season of Christmas we celebrate the birth of Jesus. Read the rebus, or picture story, about Jesus' birth.

Long ago,  and Joseph came into the town of Bethlehem. Mary rode on the back of a . They stayed in a stable. There,  was born. Some shepherds were watching their . An  came to them. The angel told the shepherds about the special baby. The shepherds went and found the baby Jesus in a .

Share the rebus story of the birth of Jesus with a younger child.

Telling the Christmas Story

Jesus, we thank you for coming to be with us. Amen.

Catholics love the Christmas story. We place figures in a lifelike display that retells the story. We call this display a crèche. It is also called a Nativity scene or a manger scene.

All during the Christmas season, we can visit the crèche in our church. When we do this, we think about the birth of Jesus. The figure of the baby Jesus is put into the manger on Christmas Day.

Long ago Saint Francis set up the first crèche near a village in Italy. The manger scene was in a cave with live animals. People went there to pray. The crèche helped them learn the story of Jesus' birth in a way they would not forget.

Lent: Ash Wednesday

Make known to me your ways, LORD;
teach me your paths.

Psalm 25:4

Marked with Jesus' Sign

We begin Mass by making the Sign of the Cross. This prayer reminds us of our faith.

The cross is an important symbol to Christians. Jesus died on a cross for our sins. We display the cross as a sign of our belief in Jesus as our Savior. During Lent we think about the meaning of the cross for our lives.

ACTIVITY

On this cross write one thing you will do for someone during Lent. Then decorate and color the cross.

The First Day of Lent

Ash Wednesday is the first day of Lent. On this day we gather in church and are marked with ashes. The priest, deacon, or another parish minister dips his or her thumb into the ashes, then traces a cross on our foreheads. The cross of ashes reminds us to try to follow Jesus more closely.

The first time you were marked with the cross was at your Baptism. Your parents and godparents marked you with the sign of the cross. A priest or deacon anointed your head with oil, making the sign of the cross. At Baptism, you became a member of the Catholic Church. Catholics pray the Sign of the Cross to remember Jesus' love for everyone.

Jesus, we belong to you. Help us live each day as your followers. Amen.

Lent: Forty Days

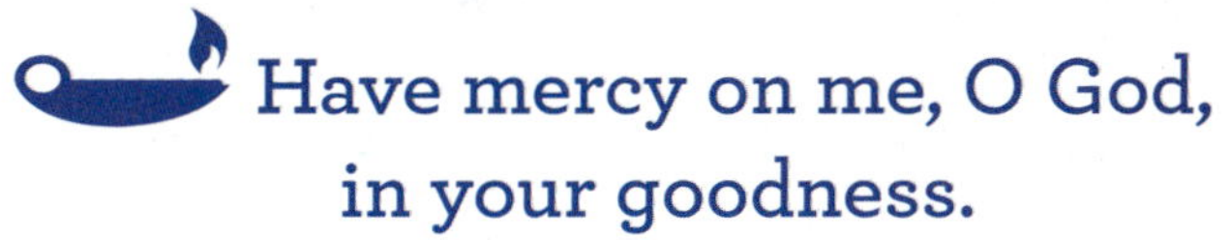

**Have mercy on me, O God,
in your goodness.**

Based on Psalm 51:3

Time For Prayer

During Lent, we remember how Jesus spent time in prayer.

Jesus calls us to think and pray as he did.

- We pray to **ask God** to help us and others.
- We pray to **praise** God's goodness.
- We pray to **thank** God for our blessings.

ACTIVITY

Think about how you will pray during Lent. Complete each sentence below.

I will ask God to help me

____.

I will praise God for

____.

I will thank God for

____

____.

The Forty Days of Lent

*Dear Jesus,
help me to grow
closer to you
through
my prayers.
Amen.*

The season of Lent lasts for forty days. We spend this time getting ready for the great feast of Easter.

Lent is a time to ask questions. We could say that Lent is an "examination of conscience" for forty days. Am I acting the way a member of Jesus' Church should act? Do I show care and kindness to other people? In what ways should I be more loving to others?

During Lent the readings at Mass tell stories about the life of Jesus. We hear about important things that Jesus taught his followers.

During Lent we try to become better followers of Jesus. We try to show more love for other people. We do good works in the name of Jesus. We pray that the Holy Spirit will help us make good choices. When we do these things, we show our love for God and for one another.

Holy Week

Jesus said, "Take this bread and eat it. This is my Body. I give it to you."

Based on Matthew 26:26

The Three Days Before Easter

During Holy Week we celebrate three very holy days. Read again Jesus' words at the top of this page. Jesus said this on Holy Thursday at the Last Supper. On Good Friday we remember Jesus dying for us. We think of new life at the Easter Vigil and on Easter Sunday.

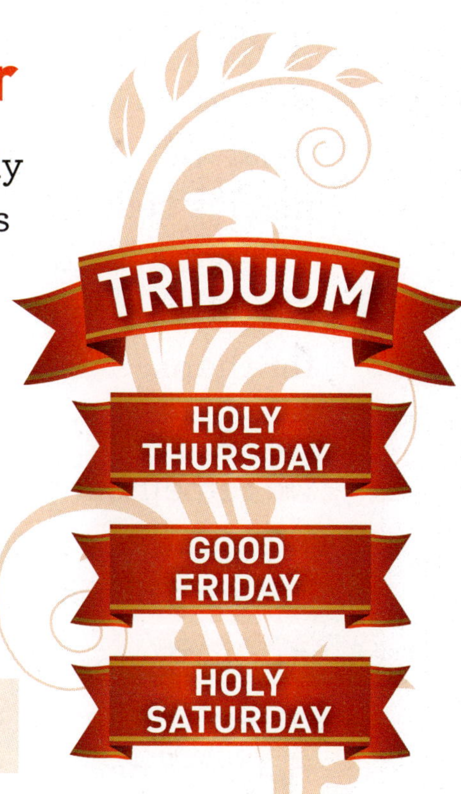

ACTIVITY

Write the correct day under each sentence.

Holy Thursday   Good Friday   Holy Saturday

We remember the Last Supper.

____

We remember the day Jesus died on the Cross.

____

We begin to celebrate Jesus' rising to new life.

____

Three Days Before Easter

The three very holy days before Easter are called the Easter Triduum. *Triduum* means "three days."

On Holy Thursday we remember the special meal that Jesus shared with his followers. This meal is called the Last Supper. Jesus gave his followers his Body and Blood in the Eucharist. He did this to show his love and concern for them.

Good Friday is another holy day. On Good Friday we remember the suffering and Death of Jesus. We remember that Jesus died on the Cross because of his love for us.

At the Easter Vigil on Holy Saturday night we begin our Easter celebration. We celebrate Jesus' rising to new life. We begin our new life in the Risen Christ.

Dear Jesus, your love for all people never ends. Thank you for loving us today and always. Amen.

Easter

"I have seen the Lord. He is alive!"
Based on John 20:18

Words of Joy

We can show we are happy and filled with joy in many ways. Sometimes we sing. Sometimes we dance. Sometimes we even shout and jump up and down. We might even give someone a great big hug!

We also show our joy in the words we use. These words let others know just how happy we are.

ACTIVITY

Circle the words below that you might use to show you are filled with joy.

Alleluia! Jesus Is Risen!

Easter is our most important feast. On Easter we celebrate the Good News that Jesus is not dead.

Jesus is alive! He is with us today!

Our parish community gathers at Mass. We sing songs filled with joy. We pray prayers of thanksgiving. We thank God for giving new life to Jesus.

We sing "Alleluia" to show how happy we are. Jesus has risen! Alleluia is our Easter word of joy and peace. During Lent, our church community does not sing "Alleluia." But now it is Easter, the Resurrection, our greatest feast of the Church year. We pray and sing "Alleluia." We listen to the Word of God that tells of Jesus' new life. We are happy and filled with God's joy.

Jesus, you
are risen from
the dead.
Alleluia! Alleluia!
Amen.

Pentecost Sunday

"... [Y]ou will receive power when the holy Spirit comes upon you, ..."
Acts 1:8

Sharing Good News

Sometimes we hear more bad news than good news. We need to hear and read about more good things happening in our world. Good news gives us hope. It brings us happiness and peace.

ACTIVITY

Think about some good news you have heard. Write a headline for a story about good news.

Great Weather Today!

The GOOD NEWS

Come, Holy Spirit!

Holy Spirit, you came to guide the followers of Jesus. Help and guide us today. Amen.

After his Resurrection, Jesus told his followers to wait for a special promise from God. They waited in Jerusalem with Jesus' mother, Mary. Crowds of people began coming to Jerusalem. It was time for the Jewish festival of **Pentecost**. Jews had come from faraway places to worship in the Temple.

As Jesus' followers prayed together, a sound like a strong wind filled the room. Then, small flames of fire rested on each person. The Holy Spirit came to give them strength.

They started telling people about Jesus. They shared the Good News with many people. The number of Jesus' followers grew and grew.

Based on Acts 2:1–47

The Feast of Pentecost Sunday comes fifty days after Easter. On Pentecost, we celebrate the birthday of the Church. The Holy Spirit remains with the Church today. The Holy Spirit makes us strong, helping us to follow Jesus.

Mary

Hail, Mary, full of grace. The Lord is with thee.

Based on Luke 1:28

The Hail Mary

Our Church honors the saints with our prayers. Our greatest saint is Mary. The prayer the Church most often prays to honor Mary is the Hail Mary.

ACTIVITY

Pray the words of the Hail Mary slowly. Fill in the missing words.

Hail, Mary, full of ________________,
the Lord is with thee.
Blessed art thou among women
and ________________ is the fruit
of thy womb, Jesus.
Holy Mary, ________________ of God,
pray for us sinners
now and at the hour of our death.
________________.

*Dear Mary,
pray that I
will always
love and trust
in God,
as you did.
Amen.*

A Prayer to Honor Mary

God's angel, Gabriel, came to Mary and said, "Hail, Mary. The Lord is with you!" The angel told Mary that she would give birth to God's own Son. "The Holy Spirit and the power of the Most High will come over you." Mary loved and trusted God. She said "yes" with these words, "May it be done as you say."

Later Mary went to see Elizabeth, her cousin. Elizabeth said to Mary, "Blessed are you among women, and blessed is the fruit of your womb, Jesus."

Based on Luke 1:26–42

The words of the angel and of Elizabeth are in the Hail Mary. We honor Mary, the Mother of God, with this prayer. We ask Mary to pray for us now. We ask her to pray for us always. The Hail Mary is also part of another special prayer, the Rosary.

Our Lady of the Rosary

Our Catholic Church honors Mary in special ways. The Rosary is a special prayer that honors Mary.

Learn to pray the Rosary.

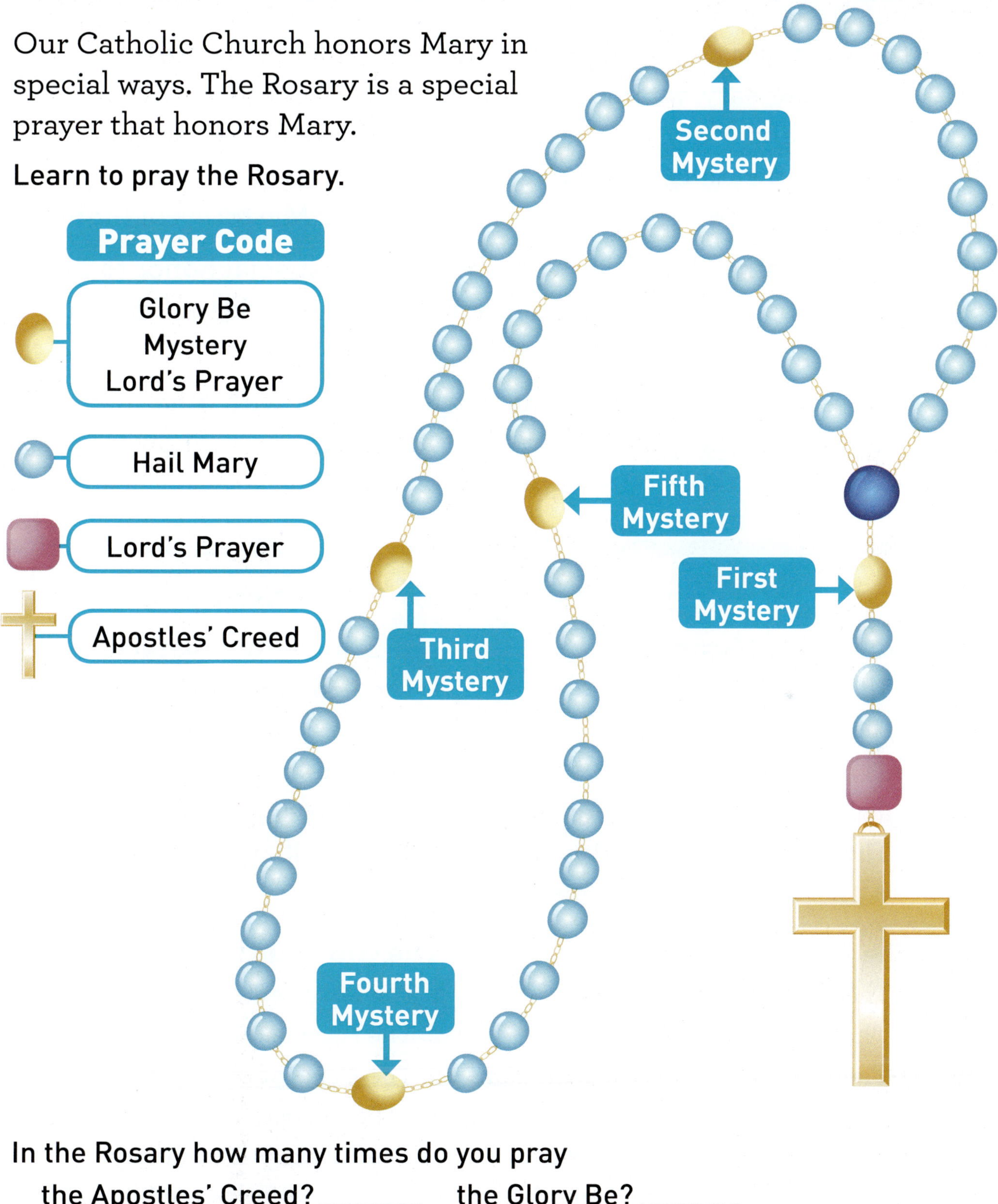

In the Rosary how many times do you pray

the Apostles' Creed? ______ the Glory Be? ______

the Lord's Prayer? ______ the Hail Mary? ______

How many mysteries are there in each set? ______

The Mysteries of the Rosary

The Rosary is a special prayer that honors Mary. When we pray the Rosary, we remember important times in the lives of Jesus and Mary. These are called mysteries. In 2002, Saint John Paul II added five new mysteries to the Rosary. They are called the Luminous Mysteries, or Mysteries of Light.

In the months of May and October, we pay special honor to Mary. On October 7, the Church celebrates the Memorial of Our Lady of the Rosary.

We can pray the Rosary alone. We can pray it with other people. We can pray the Rosary silently or aloud. No matter how we pray, Mary always takes our prayers to God.

The Mysteries of the Rosary

The Joyful Mysteries

1. The Annunciation
2. The Visitation
3. The Nativity
4. The Presentation in the Temple
5. The Finding of the Child Jesus After Three Days in the Temple

The Sorrowful Mysteries

1. The Agony in the Garden
2. The Scourging at the Pillar
3. The Crowning with Thorns
4. The Carrying of the Cross
5. The Crucifixion and Death

The Luminous Mysteries

1. The Baptism at the Jordan
2. The Miracle at Cana
3. The Proclamation of the Kingdom and the Call to Conversion
4. The Transfiguration of Jesus
5. The Institution of the Eucharist

The Glorious Mysteries

1. The Resurrection
2. The Ascension
3. The Descent of the Holy Spirit at Pentecost
4. The Assumption of Mary
5. The Crowning of the Blessed Virgin as Queen of Heaven and Earth

Our Catholic Heritage

What Catholics Believe

How Catholics Worship

How Catholics Live

How Catholics Pray

What Catholics Believe

To have faith is to believe in God. We come to know God through the Bible and the teachings of the Church.

About
The Bible

The Bible is a special book about God. Bible stories tell how God loves and cares for all people. You can learn more about the Bible on pages 17–21.

About
The Trinity

There is only one God. There is One God in Three Divine Persons—the Father, the Son, and the Holy Spirit. We call the Three Divine Persons the **Holy Trinity**.

God the Father

God is our heavenly Father. He loves and cares for us. God created everything out of love.

Jesus Christ

Jesus Christ is God's own Son. Jesus became a man. He died on the Cross and rose from the dead for us. Jesus is our Savior. He saves us from sin.

The Holy Spirit

The Holy Spirit is also God. We receive the Holy Spirit at Baptism. He gives us special gifts to share with others.

About
The Catholic Church

We are Catholics. We are the People of God. As followers of Jesus we celebrate the Sacraments. We share the gifts of the Holy Spirit. We pray to God in many ways. We can pray with others or by ourselves.

The Catholic Church is our faith community. Our faith community shares the Good News about Jesus. Helping and caring for others is a part of being Catholic.

About
Mary

God blessed Mary in a special way. God chose Mary to be the Mother of Jesus. Mary loved and cared for God's Son, Jesus.

We call Mary "Mother," too. She is our Mother in Heaven. Like a good mother, Mary loves and cares for us. The Rosary is a special prayer to honor Mary.

Mary is our greatest saint. Saints show us how to follow Jesus.

About
New Life Forever

Jesus teaches us to act with love. When we act with love, we will be happy with God in Heaven after we die. **Heaven** is happiness with God forever.

How Catholics Worship

Worship is giving honor, thanks, and praise to God. We worship when we pray and when we celebrate the Eucharist. We worship when we celebrate the Sacraments.

About
The Sacraments

Sacraments are celebrations of God's love for us. We celebrate that we share in Jesus' new life. There are Seven Sacraments.

Baptism is the Sacrament that welcomes us as new members of the Church. We receive the Holy Spirit. Baptism takes away all sin. We share in the new life of Jesus.

Confirmation is the Sacrament in which the Holy Spirit makes our faith in Jesus Christ stronger. The Holy Spirit helps us share the Good News about Jesus.

Eucharist is the Sacrament in which we share a holy meal and celebrate and make present again Jesus' sacrifice on the Cross. The Eucharist is God's gift of love to us. We thank God for giving us the Body and Blood of Christ that we receive in Holy Communion.

Penance and Reconciliation is the Sacrament that celebrates the gift of God's forgiveness. It also celebrates the gift of God's love for us. We say we are sorry for our sins. We promise to turn away from sin. God shows mercy and forgives us.

Anointing of the Sick is a Sacrament of Healing. It is the Sacrament of Christ's peace and forgiveness, if the person cannot go to Confession. People who are sick, elderly, or dying receive this Sacrament.

The Sacrament of **Holy Orders** celebrates priests, deacons, and bishops. These baptized men are called by God to serve others in the Church.

Matrimony is the Sacrament that celebrates the love of a baptized man and a baptized woman for each other. A husband and wife share God's love with their children. They serve one another and the community.

About Reconciliation

We can celebrate the Sacrament of Penance and Reconciliation with our parish community. We know that we all need God's forgiveness and mercy.

Introductory Rites

We sing a song of praise. The priest welcomes us and prays with us.

The Word of God

We listen to readings from the Bible. The priest helps us understand the readings.

Examination of Conscience

We think about our words and actions. We ask the Holy Spirit to help us turn away from sin. We pray the Lord's Prayer together.

Rite of Reconciliation

We pray a prayer of sorrow. We each go alone to confess our sins to the priest. We talk about the words or actions for which we are sorry. Then we ask for forgiveness. We receive a penance. The priest gives us absolution—the forgiveness of God.

Proclamation of Praise

We praise and thank God. We are happy that God forgives us. We are happy that he loves us always and forever.

Concluding Prayer of Thanksgiving

The priest offers a blessing for us. We sing a song of praise.

Steps to Reconciliation

When we receive the Sacrament of Penance and Reconciliation we meet with the priest. We follow these steps:

1. Examination of Conscience

Before I go to confession, I examine my conscience. I ask myself some important questions. Have I hurt other people or myself? Have I done hurtful things on purpose?

2. Welcome

The priest welcomes me. I make the Sign of the Cross and say, "In the name of the Father, and of the Son, and of the Holy Spirit. Amen."

3. Reading

The priest may read a story from the Bible. The story will be about God's love, mercy, and forgiveness.

4. Confession of Sins

The priest listens as I talk. I explain my sins. I tell the priest how I may have hurt myself or others.

5. Penance

The priest asks me to say a prayer or do an act of goodness. This penance will help me make up for what I have done wrong.

6. Prayer of Sorrow

I tell God I am sorry for my sins. I say a prayer of sorrow. This prayer is called the Act of Contrition.

GO TO page 16 for the Act of Contrition.

7. Absolution

The priest says a prayer in the name of the Church. Then he asks God to forgive my sins. The priest gives me absolution, which is the forgiveness of God.

The priest says, "I absolve you from your sins in the name of the Father, and of the Son, and of the Holy Spirit."

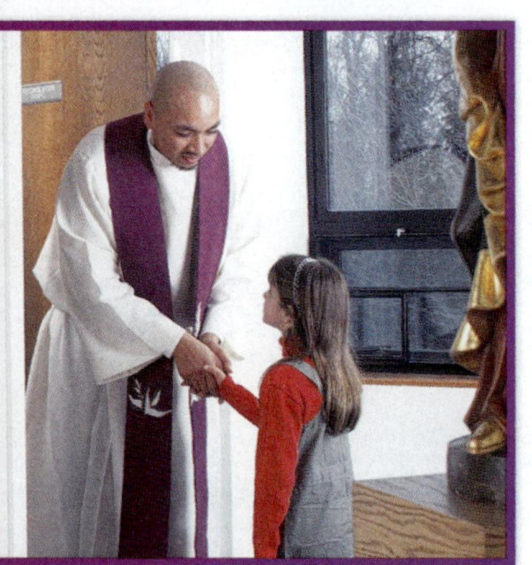

8. Prayer of Thanksgiving and Dismissal

With the priest, I thank God for being forgiven. This is called the Prayer of Thanksgiving. Then the priest says to me, "Go in peace."

I answer, "Amen."

About

The Mass

The Mass is the best way to worship God.

1. Our celebration begins. The priest and the other ministers walk in a procession to the altar. We stand and sing a song of welcome.

2. We make the Sign of the Cross. The priest welcomes us with the words, "The Lord be with you." We answer, "And with your spirit."

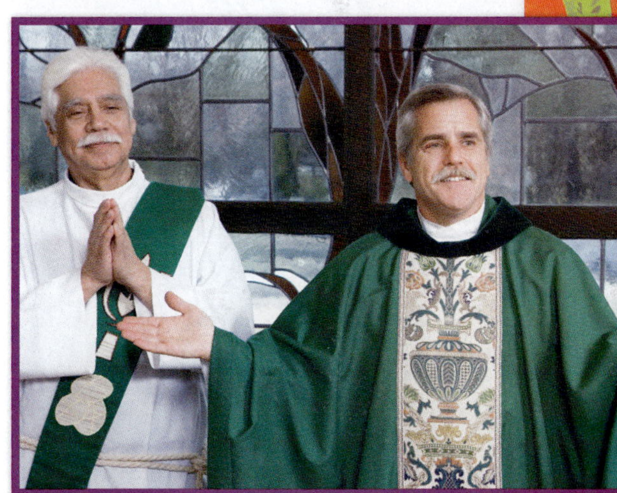

3. We remember our sins. We ask God and other people to forgive us. We then sing or say the Gloria. It is a prayer of praise and thanks.

The Liturgy of the Word

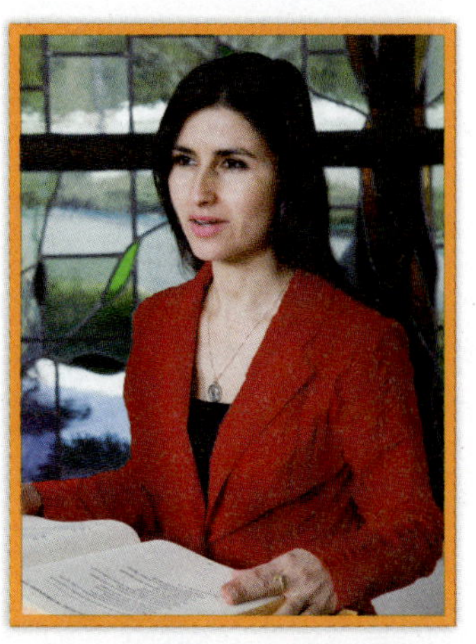

4. We listen to the Word of God in readings from the Bible. After the first two readings we say, "Thanks be to God." We sing responses to a Bible psalm between the first two readings.

5. We stand to sing "Alleluia." The priest or deacon reads the Gospel story. We listen to the Good News of Jesus. We say, "Praise to you, Lord Jesus Christ."

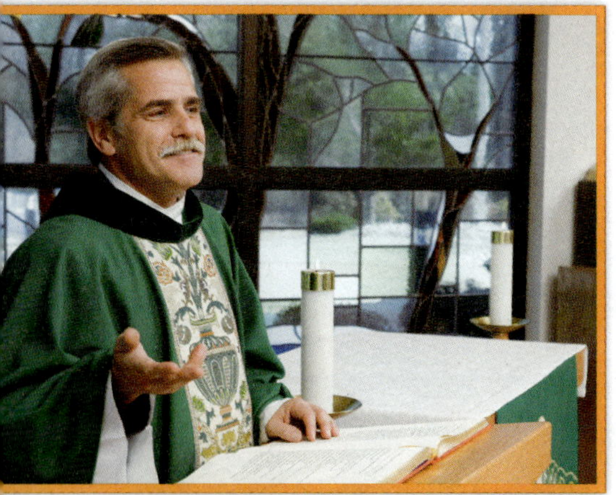

6. The priest or deacon gives a talk called a homily. It helps us understand the Bible readings.

7. We stand and pray the Nicene or the Apostles' Creed. We say what we believe as Catholics. In the Prayer of the Faithful we ask God to help all of the People of God.

The Liturgy of the Eucharist

8. We bring gifts of bread and wine to the altar. We prepare to share a special meal with Jesus. We remember that Jesus always loves us.

9. The priest offers our gifts of bread and wine to God. We thank and praise God for all of our blessings. We especially thank God for the gift of Jesus.

10. The priest prays as Jesus did at the Last Supper. Through the words of the priest and the power of Holy Spirit, bread and wine become the Body and Blood of Jesus Christ.

11. We say a prayer of faith. We may say, "We proclaim your Death, O Lord, and profess your Resurrection until you come again." The priest says a prayer to praise God. We answer, "Amen."

12. We pray the Lord's Prayer together. This is the prayer that Jesus taught us to pray.

13. We offer one another a Sign of Peace. This sign reminds us to live as Jesus teaches us to live.

14. We receive the Body and Blood of Christ at Communion. We say, "Amen." Together we sing a Communion song. We give thanks and praise for the gift of Jesus Christ in the Eucharist.

15. The priest gives us God's blessing. We go in peace to love and serve all people.

How Catholics Live

God wanted to help everyone lead good lives. God gave us the Ten Commandments. Jesus teaches us how to live. Jesus gives us the Holy Spirit to help us make good choices.

About
The Great Commandment

The **Great Commandment** tells us how to love God and other people. Jesus said, "Love God with all your heart. Love your neighbor as yourself."

Based on Mark 12:30–31; Deuteronomy 6:5

About
The New Commandment

Jesus gave us the **New Commandment**. He said, "Love one another as I have loved you."

Based on John 13:34

God wants us to be loving people. We show our love by caring for all living things. When we do not treat others with love, we sin. Sin is turning away from God. It is choosing to do hurtful things on purpose. The Holy Spirit helps us stay away from sin and choose what is good.

 **Scripture Verse**

"I give you a new commandment: love one another."

John 13:34

About

The Beatitudes

The Bible tells us a story of Jesus as a great teacher. The story is called The Sermon on the Mount (see Matthew 5:1–10). Jesus taught his followers eight Beatitudes. The Beatitudes tell us how to live.

The Beatitudes	Living the Beatitudes
Happy are the poor in spirit. The Reign of God is theirs.	We are poor in spirit when we know that we need God more than anything else.
Happy are the sorrowful. They will be comforted.	When we are in sorrow or hurting, we trust that God and others will comfort us.
Happy are the gentle. They will receive all that God has promised.	We are gentle and patient with others. We believe we will share in God's promises.
Happy are those who hunger and thirst for justice. They will be satisfied.	We try to be fair and just toward others. We share what we have with those in need.
Happy are those who show mercy. They will receive mercy.	We forgive those who are unkind to us. We accept the forgiveness of others.
Happy are the pure of heart. They will see God.	We try to keep God first in our lives. We believe we will live forever with God.
Happy are the peacemakers. They will be called the children of God.	We try to bring God's peace to the world. When we live peacefully, we are known as God's children.
Happy are those who are treated unfairly for doing what is right. The Kingdom of Heaven will belong to them.	We try to do what is right even when we are teased or insulted. We believe we will be with God forever.

Based on Matthew 5:1–10

About

The Ten Commandments

We can find God's Commandments in the Bible (see Exodus 20:1–17). The Ten Commandments help us know right from wrong. They are God's laws. When we live by them, we grow in holiness.

Living God's Laws

1. I, the Lord, am your God. You shall not have other gods besides me.
2. You shall not take the name of the Lord, your God, in vain.
3. Remember to keep holy the Lord's day.
4. Honor your father and mother.
5. You shall not kill.
6. You shall not commit adultery.
7. You shall not steal.
8. You shall not bear false witness against your neighbor.
9. You shall not covet your neighbor's wife.
10. You shall not covet anything that belongs to your neighbor.

Based on Exodus 20:1–17

Catholics can

- help at Mass by reading Scripture, leading songs, or giving Holy Communion to people.
- share the Gospel message of Jesus.
- treat all people fairly.

About
Vocations

God calls each of us to live our lives in a special way to serve the Church and one another. This is called our **vocation**. The Church names four vocations in which God may call us to serve.

1. Bishops and priests are ordained to lead the Catholic community. They celebrate the Sacraments and preach God's Word. Deacons are ordained ministers too. They can read the Gospel and preach homilies. They celebrate Baptism and Matrimony. They serve people in need.

2. Religious sisters and brothers are lay people who serve others. They live simple lives with one another. They also obey God's law and the rules of their communities. They give themselves to serving the Church in many ways.

3. Some lay people are called to the vocation of marriage. Their family life is a sign of Christ's love for the Church.

4. Others choose to be single. They do not become religious brothers or sisters. They promise never to marry. They choose to serve the Church in many ways and build up the Kingdom of God.

You are still called by your Baptism to live in a way that builds up the Church. Jesus calls you to find a way to serve the Church and live for others as he did.

About

Religious Sisters

Religious sisters have a special vocation. They belong to groups called *communities*. They spend their lives working for God and for all of God's people.

Some sisters are teachers. Some sisters work with the poor, the sick, and the elderly. Still others are missionaries. They bring the Good News of the Gospel to people in countries all over the world.

Each religious sister makes important promises. She promises to love and serve God. She promises to live a simple life. She promises to be an example of what is good. And she promises to show others how to live a good Christian life.

How Catholics Pray

Prayer is talking and listening to God. We can pray anywhere and at any time. God is everywhere. God always hears our prayers.

About
Kinds of Prayer

When we pray, we spend time with God. We need to pray every day. Everyone can pray. There are many reasons to pray. We can pray for someone we love. We can say a prayer of sorrow to God. We can pray just to share our thoughts with God. We can say, "I love you, God." We can pray to say, "Thank you, God."

We can pray with others, as we do at Mass. We can pray by saying a prayer quietly in our hearts. We can pray by sitting very still. We can just listen to the sounds around us.

A dance, a song, and a smile can each be a prayer. If our hearts are filled with love, then our actions become special prayers.

About

The Lord's Prayer

The Lord's Prayer is a very special prayer. It is a prayer to God, our loving Father. Jesus taught us the words to say. In this prayer we honor God. We pray that what God wants for us will be done. We ask God for what we need.

Our Father, who art in heaven, hallowed be thy name;

God is our Father. We praise God. We pray that everyone will say God's name with love.

thy kingdom come,

Jesus told us about God's kingdom. God's kingdom is happiness with God forever. We pray that everyone in the world will know God's love.

thy will be done on earth as it is in heaven.

We pray that everyone will live in peace. We pray that everyone will follow God's Word.

Give us this day our daily bread,

God is good. God cares for us. We pray for our needs and for the needs of others.

and forgive us our trespasses, as we forgive those who trespass against us;

We ask God to forgive us when we sin. We remember that we must forgive others, too.

and lead us not into temptation,

We pray that God will help us make good choices.

but deliver us from evil.

We pray that God will protect us from things that may harm us.

Amen.

Our "Amen" says that Jesus' prayer is our prayer, too.

Write-in Glossary

Absolution (page 81)
______________ is God's forgiveness given through the priest in the Sacrament of Penance and Reconciliation.

Act of Contrition (page 101)
The ______ of ______________ is a prayer that tells God we are sorry for our sins.

Anointing of the Sick (page 263)
______________ of the ______ is a Sacrament of Healing. It is the Sacrament of Christ's peace and forgiveness, if the person cannot go to Confession. People who are sick, elderly, or dying receive this Sacrament.

Baptism (page 39)
The Sacrament of ______________ washes away sin and welcomes new members to the Church.

Bible (page 18)
The ______________ is God's Word written by human writers. This holy book helps us learn about God's great love for us. The Bible is also called Sacred Scripture.

bless (page 227)
To ______________ means to ask for God's good will toward someone.

blessing (page 227)
A ______________ asks for God's gifts for others or for ourselves. It is a sign of God's love.

Confession (page 80)
______ is talking about or confessing our sins to a priest in the Sacrament of Penance and Reconciliation.

Confirmation (page 262)
______ is the Sacrament in which the Holy Spirit makes our faith in Jesus Christ stronger.

conscience (page 71)
Our ______ is our ability to know right from wrong.

Contrition (page 101)
______ is sorrow for doing wrong and wanting to stay away from sin.

creation (page 113)
God made all ______ good.

Eucharist (page 165)
In the Sacrament of the ______ we receive the Body and Blood of Christ. The Eucharist is a sacrifice and a sacred meal of Christ's Body and Blood.

Free will (page 71)
______ ______ is the freedom God gives us to choose what to do.

Gospel (page 18)
The ______ is the Good News of Jesus in the Bible. The four Gospels tell the Good News of Jesus' life and teachings.

Grace (page 81)
______________ is the gift of God's life within us that fills us with his love.

Great Commandment (page 271)
The ______________ ______________ tells us how to love God and other people.

Hallowed (page 185)
______________ is another word for holy.

Heaven (page 261)
______________ is happiness with God forever.

holy (page 49)
To be ______________ means to be like God.

Holy Communion (page 165)
We receive the Body and Blood of Christ in ______________ ______________.

Holy Orders (page 207)
In the Sacrament of ______________ ______________ bishops, priests, and deacons are ordained to special service in the Church.

homily (page 123)
A ____________ is a talk given by a priest or deacon. It helps us understand the readings we have just heard, our faith, or the feast we are celebrating.

Justice (page 217)
____________ means treating people fairly.

Liturgy of the Eucharist (page 164)
The ____________ of the ____________ is the second part of the Mass.

Liturgy of the Word (page 123)
The ____________ of the ____________ is when we listen to God's Word from the Bible at Mass.

Lord's Prayer (page 185)
The ____________ ____________ is the prayer that Jesus taught us.

Mass (page 29)
The ____________ is a holy meal Jesus shares with us. At Mass, we offer praise and sacrifice to God and can receive the Body and Blood of Jesus..

Matrimony (page 207)
In the Sacrament of ____________ a baptized man and a baptized woman promise to be faithful to each other for their whole lives.

mortal sin
(page 91)

A ________ ________ is the most serious kind of sin. It separates us completely from God's grace.

New Commandment
(page 175)

In the ________ ________ Jesus tells us to love one another as he loves us.

Nicene Creed
(page 123)

The ________ ________ tells the important beliefs of the Catholic faith.

Original Sin
(page 39)

________ ________ is the sin of the first man and woman, Adam and Eve.

Peace
(page 217)

________ means getting along with others.

penance
(page 100)

A ________ is a prayer or an act to make up for the harm caused by sin.

Penance and Reconciliation
(page 81)

________ and ________ is a Sacrament of Healing that celebrates God's love and forgiveness.

People of God
(page 29)

The ________ of ________ are followers of Jesus Christ.

Praise
(page 59)

________________ is a joyful type of prayer. It celebrates God's goodness.

Prayer
(page 59)

________________ is talking to and listening to God.

Prayer of the Faithful
(page 143)

During the ________________ of the ________________ we pray for the needs of the Church and of all people. This prayer is the last part of the Liturgy of the Word.

Psalms
(page 59)

________________ are prayers from the Bible that are often sung.

Resurrection
(page 155)

The ________________ is Jesus' being raised from the dead to new life.

Sacraments
(page 39)

________________ are special signs of God's love and presence that bring us his grace.

Sacred Scripture
(page 18)

The Bible is called ________________ ________________ ________________.

sacrifice (page 155)
A ______________ is a special gift that is given out of love.

Saints (page 49)
______________ are people who showed great love for God and others and died filled with God's grace. They live with him now in Heaven.

savior (page 155)
A ______________ is someone who rescues others.

Service (page 133)
______________ means doing work that helps others.

sin (page 71)
To ______________ is to choose to do hurtful things on purpose. Sin is disobeying God.

Son of God (page 113)
Jesus is the ______________ of ______________. He is true God and true man.

Spiritual gifts (page 196)
______________ ______________ are given to us by the Holy Spirit. We use them to help others and ourselves.

temptation (page 185) A ______________ is wanting to do something that is wrong.

Ten Commandments (page 90) The ______________ ______________ are God's laws. They help us to know how to lead good lives.

Trespasses (page 185) ______________ are sins or wrongs.

venial sin (page 91) A ______________ ______________ is a less serious sin. It weakens our love for God and others.

vocation (page 274) A ______________ is God's call to us to live our lives in a special way to serve the Church and one another.

Word of God (page 113) The ______________ of ______________ is God speaking to us in the Bible.

Works of Mercy (page 133) The ______________ of ______________ tell how to take care of the needs of others.

Index

Credits

COVER ILLUSTRATION: Richard Johnson/ The Organisation

SCRIPTURE ILLUSTRATION: Marcin Piwowarski/ Bright Group International; 17; 18; 19; 28-29; 46; 48-49; 56; 58-59; 68; 70-71; 78; 90-91;100-101; 110; 112-113; 120; 122-123; 130; 132-133; 142-143; 152; 154-155; 172; 174-175; 184-185; 194; 196-197; 204; 214; 216-217; 224; 226-227

IMAGE CREDITS

9 ©JupiterImages/Getty, ©P Deliss/Getty; 10 ©Maria Jimenez/RCL Benziger; 11 ©Lifeway Collection/GoodSalt; 12 ©Vivian Imbruglia/www.sacredimageicons.com; 13 ©QBS Learning Illustrations; 14 ©MBI/Alamy Stock Photo; 15 ©Maria Jimenez/RCL Benziger, ©RCL Benziger; 16 ©EricVega/Getty; 21 ©RCL Benziger; 23 ©BibleLandPictures.com/Alamy Stock Photo, ©Jupiterimages/Thinkstock; 24 ©Bill Wittman; 25 ©RCL Benziger, ©DEA/M. SEEMULLER/ Getty; 26 ©Diane Paterson/RCL Benziger, ©Gene Plaisted, OSC/The Crosiers; 27 ©Hero Images Inc./Alamy Stock Photo; 30 ©RCL Benziger; 32 ©Rawpixel Ltd/Thinkstock; 34 ©Marmaduke St. John/Alamy Stock Photo; 35 ©Bill Wittman, ©Tracy L. Christianson/portraitsofsaints.com; 36 ©Bill Wittman, ©National Gallery, London, UK/Bridgeman Images; 37 ©QBS Learning Illustrations; 38 ©QBS Learning Illustrations, ©Rob Melnychuk/Getty, ©Bill Wittman; 39 ©Marmaduke St. John/Alamy Stock Photo, ©Bill Wittman; 40 ©INSADCO Photography/Alamy Stock Photo; 41 ©QBS Learning Illustrations; 42 ©Photononstop / Alamy Stock Photo; 44 ©Bill Wittman; 45 ©RCLBenziger, ©Gene Plaisted, OSC/ The Crosiers; 46 ©RCL Benziger; 47 ©Monkey Business Images/Thinkstock, ©Imagestate Media Partners Limited - Impact Photos/Alamy Stock Photo, ©Myrleen Pearson / PhotoEdit—All rights reserved.; 50 ©RCL Benziger; 52 ©Tetra Images—Chris Hackett/Getty; 54 ©StockbyteThinkstock; 55 ©Zurijeta/Shutterstock, ©DEA/VENERANDA BIBLIOTECA AMBROSIANA/Getty; 56 ©RCL Benziger; 57 ©QBS Learning Illustrations; 60 ©Bill Wittman; 62 ©Visage / Alamy Stock Photo; 64 ©Bill Wittman, ©QBS Learning Illustrations; 65 ©Sylvain Grandadam/Getty, ©Bill Wittman; 66 ©Blend Images/Alamy Stock Photo; 67 ©Robert Matton AB/Alamy Stock Photo, ©QBS Learning Illustrations; 68 ©Rembrandt Harmensz. van Rijn (1606-69)/State Hermitage Museum, St. Petersburg, Russia/Bridgeman Images; 72 ©RCL Benziger; 73 ©QBS Learning Illustrations; 74 ©George Coppock/Getty; 76 ©RCLBenziger, ©QBS Learning Illustrations; 77 ©RCL Benziger, ©Gene Plaisted, OSC/The Crosiers; 78 ©Getty Images/Handout; 79 ©QBS Learning Illustrations; 80 ©Bill Wittman; 82 ©Morella Fuenmayor/RCL Benziger; 84 ©RubberBall Productions/Getty; 86 ©OJO Images Ltd /Alamy Stock Photo; 87 ©Westend61/Getty, ©Chris Howes/Wild Places Photography/Alamy Stock Photo; 88 ©Jon Arnold Images Ltd/Alamy Stock Photo, ©Jubilee Year of Mercy; 89 © Blend Images / Alamy Stock Photo; 92 ©RCLBenziger; 93 ©QBS Learning Illustrations; 94 ©Russell Monk/Getty; 96 ©Tetra Images/Alamy Stock Photo; 97 ©RCLBenziger, ©Holmes Garden Photos/Alamy Stock Photo; 98 ©Noah Gutierrez/ noahpgutierrez@yahoo.com, ©Everett Collection, Inc.; 99 © David Laurens/Getty, © digitalskillet/ Getty, ©TuTheLens/Thinkstock; 102 ©Providence Collection/GoodSalt; 104 ©Stockbyte/Getty; 106 ©Bill Wittman, ©RCL Benziger; 107 ©Avalon_ Studio/Getty, Copyright ©Myrleen Pearson / PhotoEdit—All rights reserved.; 108 ©Design Pics Inc /Alamy Stock Photo; 109 ©RCL Benziger, ©Tracy L. Christianson/portraitsofsaints.com; 110 ©Newberry Library, Chicago/Superstock; 114 ©Hero Images Inc./ Alamy Stock Photo; 115 ©Tom Sperling/RCL Benziger; 116 ©Andrew_ Mayovskyy/Thinkstock; 118 ©Bill Wittman; 119 ©RCL Benziger, ©Hulton Fine Art Collection/ Getty; 120 ©Macduff Everton/Corbis/VCG/ Getty; 121 ©Lawrence Migdale/Stone/Getty; 124 ©Robert Nicholas/Getty; 126 ©elenavolkova/ Thinkstock; 128 ©Bill Wittman, ©QBS Learning Illustrations; 129 ©RCL Benziger, ©Ken Welsh / Alamy Stock Photo; 130 ©Catholic News Service; 131 ©QBS Learning Illustrations; 134 ©Dorothy Stott/RCL Benziger; 136 ©Tracy L. Christianson/ portraitsofsaints.com, ©Marina113/Thinkstock; 138 ©Jeff Greenberg / Alamy Stock Photo; 139 ©RCL Benziger, ©Tyler Boley/Getty; 140 ©Gene Plaisted, OSC/The Crosiers, ©Gene Plaisted, OSC/ The Crosiers; 141 ©RCL Benziger; 144 ©Scott Peterson / Contributor/Getty, ©Christina Kennedy / Alamy Stock Photo; 146 ©leonello/Thinkstock; 148 ©Brand X Pictures/Thinkstock; 149 ©Bill Wittman, ©Zev Radovan_Jerusalem; 150 ©Visual Source Photography/RCL Benziger; 151 © RCL Benziger, ©jozef sedmak /Alamy Stock Photo; 152 ©Congregation of Holy Cross; 153 ©RCL Benziger; 156 ©Dorothy Stott/RCL Benziger; 157 ©mcherevan/Shutterstock; 158 ©Gene Plaisted, OSC/The Crosiers; 160 ©Marmaduke St. John/Alamy Stock Photo; 161 ©Tetra Images/ Alamy Stock Photo, ©INSADCO Photography/ Alamy Stock Photo; 162 ©RonandJoe/Thinkstock, ©Jurekk/Alamy Stock Photo; 163 ©QBS Learning Illustrations; 164 ©Gene Plaisted, OSC/The Crosiers; 165 ©Myrleen Pearson/PhotoEdit; 166 ©KidStock/Getty, ©Gene Plaisted, OSC/The Crosiers; 167 ©QBS Learning Illustrations; 168 ©Angela Lumsden/Getty; 170 ©Bill Wittman; 171 ©RCL Benziger, ©Tracy L. Christianson/ portraitsofsaints.com; 172 ©North Wind Picture Archives/Alamy Stock Photo; 173 ©QBS Learning Illustrations; 176 ©Design Pics Inc / Alamy Stock Photo; 178 ©RCL Benziger; 180 ©BSIP SA / Alamy Stock Photo; 181 ©Milt & Joan Mann / CameraMann International, Ltd., ©Gene Plaisted, OSC/The Crosiers; 182 ©Darrel Tank/GoodSalt, ©De Agostini Picture Library / G. Nimatallah / Bridgeman Images; 183 ©QBS Learning Illustrations; 186 ©Jupiterimages/Thinkstock; 187 ©RCL Benziger; 188 ©Andreas Karelias/ Thinkstock, ©Olena Abazid/Thinkstock; 190 ©Robert Daly/Getty; 191 ©alexeys/Thinkstock; 192 ©Kzenon/Alamy Stock Photo; 193 ©Jose Luis Pelaez Inc/Blend Images/ Alamy Stock Photo, ©DEA/A. DAGLI ORTI /Getty; 194 ©Jon Arnold Images Ltd/Alamy Stock Photo; 195 ©Corbis Super RF/Alamy Stock Photo, ©Hero Images/ Getty, ©FSG/Getty; 198 © Perry Milou/www.http://perrymilou.com; 200 ©SerrNovik/Thinkstock; 202 © Bill Wittman; 203 ©Private Collection/ Archives Charmet/Bridgeman Images; 204 ©epa european pressphoto agency b.v./Alamy Stock Photo; 205 ©Morella Fuenmayor/RCL Benziger; 206 ©Bill Wittman; 207 ©Bob Mullen/The Catholic Photographer/catholicphotographer.com, ©Bob Mullen/The Catholic Photographer/ catholicphotographer.com; 208 ©Christopher Furlong/Getty; 209 ©QBS Learning Illustrations; 210 ©Ryan McVay/Thinkstock; 212 ©Bob Mullen/ The Catholic Photographer/catholicphotographer.com; 213 ©QBS Learning Illustrations, ©The Print Collector/Print Collector/Getty Images; 214 © Michael Newman/PhotoEdit—All rights reserved.; 215 ©Donna Peronne/RCL Benziger; 218 ©Mary Wessel, ©evdakovka/Thinkstock; 219 ©RCL Benziger; 220 ©RCL Benziger, ©KathyDewar/ Getty; 222 ©Jack Hollingsworth/Thinkstock; 223 ©RCL Benziger, ©QBS Learning Illustrations; 224 ©Danita Delimont/Alamy Stock Photo; 225 ©QBS Learning Illustrations; 228 ©Fuse/Getty, ©David Buffington/Getty, ©Fuse/Getty; 230 ©Ian Allenden / Alamy Stock Photo; 232 ©Jim West/Alamy Stock Photo; 233 ©Bill Wittman; 234 ©QBS Learning Illustrations; 236 ©QBS Learning Illustrations; 237 ©QBS Learning Illustrations; 238 ©Diane Paterson/RCL Benziger; 240 ©Vivian Imbruglia/ www.sacredimageicons.com; 241 ©QBS Learning Illustrations; 242 ©Linda Weller/RCL Benziger; 243 ©RCL Benziger; 244 ©Gene Plaisted, OSC/ The Crosiers; 246 ©Bill Wittman; 247 ©Ivy Close Images / Alamy Stock Photo, ©Blend Images/Alamy Stock Photo; 248 ©kirin_photo/ Getty; 250 ©Steve Skjold / Alamy Stock Photo; 251 ©Morella Fuenmayor/RCL Benziger; 252 ©ibphotos; 253 ©Monkey Business Images/ Thinkstock, ©barbaliss/Thinkstock, ©Dan ionut Popescu/Thinkstock, © yelet/Thinkstock; 254 ©Diane Paterson/RCL Benziger; 255 ©neko92vl/ Thinkstock; 256 ©Diane Paterson/RCL Benziger; 260 ©QBS Learning Illustrations; 261 ©Roger Cracknell 01/classic/Alamy Stock Photo; 262 ©Ed Buziak / Alamy Stock Photo, ©Bill Wittman, ©robertharding / Alamy Stock Photo; 263 ©Gene Plaisted, OSC/The Crosiers, ©Bob Mullen/The Catholic Photographer/catholicphotographer.com, ©Bill Wittman, ©Bill Wittman; 264 ©Gene Plaisted, OSC/The Crosiers; 265 ©RCL Benziger; 266 ©RCL Benziger; 267 ©RCL Benziger; 268 ©RCL Benziger; 269 ©RCL Benziger; 270 ©RCL Benziger; 271 ©Gene Plaisted, OSC/The Crosiers, ©Jack Hollingsworth/Thinkstock; 274 ©Bill Wittman; 275 ©Friedrich Stark/Alamy Stock Photo; 276 ©LuckyBusiness/Thinkstock; 277 ©Grisha Bruev/Shutterstock